Writing Biography

Writing Biography

Historians & Their Craft

Edited by Lloyd E. Ambrosius

University of Nebraska Press: Lincoln & London

Library of Congress Cataloging-in-Publication Data
Writing biography : historians and their craft / edited
by Lloyd E. Ambrosius.
p. cm.
Includes bibliographical references and index.
ISBN 0-8032-1066-3 (cloth : alkaline paper)
1. Biography as a literary form. I. Ambrosius, Lloyd E.
CT21 .W735 2004 808'.06692–dc22 2003019697

Contents

Introduction

Lloyd E. Ambrosius

Between 7 and 9 September 2000, the Department of History of the University of Nebraska–Lincoln held its first Carroll R. Pauley Memorial Endowment Symposium on the topic "Biography and Historical Analysis." We invited six prominent historians in various fields to reflect on their experiences as biographers. From their different perspectives, these scholars offered their insights into the writing of biography as a form of historical analysis. Professors Shirley A. Leckie of the University of Central Florida, R. Keith Schoppa of Loyola College of Maryland, Retha M. Warnicke of Arizona State University, John Milton Cooper Jr. of the University of Wisconsin–Madison, Nell Irvin Painter of Princeton University, and Robert J. Richards of the University of Chicago presented their original scholarly papers at the symposium. This volume is the product of their work.

Chosen because of the diversity of their perspectives on the symposium's theme—a reflection of their various personal and academic backgrounds, fields of expertise, and methodological approaches—these six scholars offered a broad range of interpretations. The three women had written biographical studies of women from different social classes in England and the United States. Their subjects included U.S. soldiers' wives and a historian, English queens, and an African American slave who became a leading feminist and abolitionist. Like their female subjects, these authors focused on social issues of gender and race. Their studies shed new light on politics too. The three men had written biographical studies of men. Their subjects included a revolutionary Chinese leader, a U.S. ambassador, two U.S. presidents, and a German philosopher. While focusing on male political and intellectual leaders, they, too, addressed social issues of class, gender, and race. They, too, appreciated the cultural connections between the personal and public aspects of a subject's life.

All six scholars, notwithstanding their diversity, agreed on one central point: Biography and historical analysis are inextricably intertwined. For them, biographical studies offer a way to analyze important historical questions. Moreover, they affirmed, biographers must use the best historical methodologies, utilizing all available primary sources and interpreting them in creative ways, to reveal the life stories of subaltern as well as prominent and powerful women and men.

As requested, these six historians focused on the symposium's theme of biography and historical analysis. They analyzed the problems of conceptualization and methodology with which historians in various fields must deal. They addressed questions such as the following: How does the biographer sort out the individual's role within the larger historical context? How do biographical studies relate to other forms of history? Should historians use different approaches to biography depending upon the societies or cultures in which the subjects lived? What are the appropriate primary sources and techniques that scholars should use in writing biographies in their fields? The original contributions of this book come from the various answers that the six historians gave to these questions.

A specialist in the American West, Shirley A. Leckie argued that biography is an important form of historical analysis that can enable readers to transcend their own personal experiences and encounter another person from a different time and place. For that to occur, however, the biographer must present the subject in such a way that "a living being walks off the pages." This requires empathy to recognize both internal and external influences, both the psychological dimensions and the environmental circumstances that shaped a person's life. While retaining a certain detachment from the subject to achieve as much historical objectivity as possible, so as to distinguish between fact and fiction, the biographer must see the world from that other person's perspective. This kind of personal understanding must be fully informed by research in all available records, both public and private. When, as is often the case for women or people of color, primary sources are inadequate to answer important questions about a person's life, biographers must make creative use of whatever is available. Historian Angie Debo employed this approach in her study of Geronimo, as did Leckie in her biography of Debo. Leckie urged historians to undertake biographical studies of other historians in order to explore the "participant-observer" relationship inherent in writing biography. Along with Leon Edel, she contended that a biographer must become a participant in the world in which the subject lived but at the same time remain outside that world as a critical observer. By doing this well, Leckie concluded, historians can write biographies that enable readers to experience the lives of others. Thus biography matters as a way of providing meaningful access to other people in different times and places.

R. Keith Schoppa, whose specialty is modern China, stressed that culture and context—of both the biographers and their subjects—profoundly influence the renderings of the past that different people embrace as history. In Chinese history, he explained, the dominant understanding of relationships between individuals and groups has been quite different from that in the modern West. To avoid imposing an erroneous interpretation onto a Chinese subject's life, a Western biographer, like Schoppa himself, must therefore recognize this essential difference between the individual-group dynamics operating in the Chinese context and those operating in the West. He stressed the role of social connections and networks in defining the identity and controlling the life and death of Chinese people, such as Shen Dingyi, whom he studied. Emphasizing this difference between Chinese and Western cultures, Schoppa noted that individualism has contributed to the popularity of biography as a form of history in the West. Western cultural assumptions about individualism, which Western historians have shared, have encouraged the writing and reading of biography that features an individual rather than a group. But in China a person's identity derives from the group, from the inherited name, not from individual choice. The biographer of a Chinese subject must therefore recognize the reality of this cultural context and interpret that person's life story within the framework of social connections and networks. Schoppa illustrated this approach with his analysis of Shen's murder in 1928.

Retha M. Warnicke, a specialist in Tudor England, likewise focused on networks in English history. She suggested that the contrast between the East and the West, which Schoppa had stressed, was not so great, at least in the early modern era. Especially in women's history, she emphasized, family and kinship networks were vitally important. These connections shaped not only the lives of queens, such as Anne Boleyn and Anne of Cleves, but also the workings of politics at the Tudor court. In early modern English history, she argued, customs and rituals of the time influenced perceptions of the royal family at the time and have continued to influence the way historians since then have written about the people of the Tudor era. Traditional beliefs about gender, which privileged men over women, and about religion, which exalted Protestantism over Catholicism after the English Reformation, have remained embedded in even recent biographies. To escape these prejudices, Warnicke urged historians to reexamine their own cultural biases as they rewrite their accounts of Tudor England. Reshaping Tudor biography, which she did with Anne Boleyn and Anne of Cleves, requires historians to take a fresh look at the available historical records, recognizing the falsehoods and prejudices within these documents and reading them without imposing the traditional stereotypes onto their content. This approach, Warnicke concluded, offers new insights not only into early modern women's history but also into English history in general. It enables the biographer to contribute not only to the social and cultural understanding of Tudor England but also to its political history.

John Milton Cooper Jr., a specialist in late nineteenth- and early twentieth-century American history, shared his experiences as a biographer of Walter Hines Page and of Theodore Roosevelt and Woodrow Wilson. Like Leckie, he stressed the importance of acquiring an empathetic understanding of the subject (or subjects, in the case of a comparative biography) while not sacrificing scholarly objectivity—in other words, striking a balance between personal empathy and critical detachment. He emphasized the need for sufficient primary sources but acknowledged that historians do not always have all the documents they would like for every biographical subject. If a person did not leave behind a collection of letters, diaries, or other private papers, historians must rely on the public record. Cooper observed that a biographer's own autobiographical experiences influence the choice of a subject and the particular perspective on that person's life. He emphasized that a biographer must enter into "conversation" with the subject, so as to allow that person to speak for himself or herself. What is now called "oral history," but which existed before it was given that name, has provided a way to engage in "conversation" with the subject or with others who knew that person. Using himself as an example, Cooper illustrated the "participant-observer" relationship that Leckie, following Leon Edel, advocated. Like Warnicke, he warned against accepting interpretations that appear in the documents without first questioning the reliability and biases of the sources, such as Edward M. House's diary for the Wilson era. Cooper recommended the methodology of comparative biography to explore two or more lives that ran parallel and intersected, as did those of Presidents Roosevelt and Wilson. He recognized the limits of this approach, however. Above all, he advised historians to become biographers by doing the research and writing the life stories of other people, for there is no substitute for one's own experience.

Drawing upon her experience as the biographer of Sojourner Truth, Nell Irvin Painter, whose specialty is African American history, urged historians to use images as well as written documents. Especially in the case of subaltern subjects, for whom primary sources are typically scarce, the biographer must utilize all available materials, whether written or pictorial. She observed that in the Western intellectual tradition words have been regarded by scholars as more reliable sources of truth than pictures. This privileging of words over images, however, favors the elite over subaltern subjects, for wealthy and powerful people are more likely to leave a legacy of written documents. Because the slave Sojourner Truth, who became a leading abolitionist and feminist, was illiterate, she could not bequeath a collection of letters and diaries. She did, however, leave pictures that revealed her own presentation of herself. By using them, along with written sources from Truth's contemporaries, Painter could gain better access to the way Truth saw herself and wanted others to see her. Combining black studies and art history, Painter advocated the revival of *ut pictura poesis*, "the sisterhood of the arts," literally, "as in painting, so in poetry." From this perspective, images would not merely supplement words as accessories but complement them on an equal basis. In subaltern biography, the use of portraiture enables historians to escape the racist or sexist stereotypes that the dominant culture has imposed upon women or people of color. Painter illustrated this approach with images of Sojourner Truth, Frederick Douglass, and Duke Ellington. She compared their own carefully presented self-images with the "controlling images"—both written and pictorial—that flourished in the dominant white society. This approach to subaltern biography, Painter argued, permits the subjects to speak for themselves and presents their "symbolic webs of meaning" that words alone could not convey. Moreover, it allows historians to expand the "conversation"—using Cooper's term—to include persons other than the usually prominent white men. With this kind of creative methodology, a biographer can write the life story of an illiterate black woman as well as those of U.S. presidents.

Robert J. Richards, too, advocated the removal of artificial boundaries. In particular, he argued that biography is a necessity in the history of philosophy. He emphasized the connection between the life-changing experiences of real people, such as Friedrich Schelling, and the shifts in their thinking. Ideas do not exist and develop on their own, unconnected with the scientists or poets who conceive them, Richards stressed, although one might get this impression from traditional accounts of the history of science and philosophy. He demonstrated this point by examining the allegation against Schelling that he was somehow responsible for the premature death of Auguste Böhmer, the daughter of his lover and, later, wife, Caroline Böhmer-Schlegel. Prior to Auguste's death, probably from typhus, he had embraced the ideas of Johann Gottlieb Fichte, including his "subjective idealism." More than the other Jena Romantics with whom he was intimately associated, he had attributed the external world to the ego, making it the projection of one's own self-consciousness. After Auguste's death, however, he shifted away from that egotistical view of the world and acknowledged its own external reality. Deeply wounded by the death and the allegations, Schelling had experienced the impact of external events upon himself. He could no longer doubt their existence outside of himself or take full responsibility for these painful experiences, as Fichte's "subjective idealism" would require by its assertion that the outside world was merely a product of one's own consciousness. In other words, an intensely personal experience provided the motivation for Schelling to modify his ideas. As this case exemplifies, Richards concluded, the history of philosophy needs biography to explain the development of ideas. Emotions, not logic alone, propel changes in thinking, and thus shape the nature of intellectual history. Just as Leckie and Warnicke advocated the removal of barriers between personal and public aspects of life, building upon the insight from women's history that the personal is political, Richards adopted this approach in the history of ideas. Biography matters in this field too. Biography is thus essential in historical analysis.

All six historians focused on the multiple relationships that shape the work of historians as biographers. Their essays, which comprise the chapters in this volume, explored the overlapping connections between autobiography and biography, between truth and subjectivity, between biographers and the people they choose as subjects, between these individual subjects and their society or culture, between biographers and their own society or culture, between the personal and public aspects of the subjects' lives, and between various subjects and their legacies of historical records available to biographers. By examining all these relationships, the six historians offered insights from their own experiences as biographers into the important topic of biography and historical analysis.

Writing Biography

1. Biography Matters: Why Historians Need Well-Crafted Biographies More than Ever

Shirley A. Leckie

In September 1999, Stanley Fish, dean of the College of Liberal Arts and Sciences at the University of Illinois–Chicago, attacked modern biography as "Minutiae without Meaning" in the *New York Times*. It had fallen into this sorry state, he maintained, because the old "master narrative models" had lost their meaning for contemporary readers. These included "the providential model," based on the idea that humans, tainted by original sin, inevitably repeat the failings of Adam and Eve, and the "wheel of fortune model," which sees cycles of luck and misfortune as determining life's outcome. Hence, modern biographers furiously collect details and then "invent or fabricate a meaning," based on their "favorite hobby horse," to hold their narratives together. But, in reality, Fish argued, they are "left with little more than a collection of random incidents, and the only truth being told is the truth of contingency, of events succeeding one another in a universe of accident and chance."[1]

Since "cause and effect" remains the biographers' "stock in trade," Fish accused modern biographers of imposing on their work their own contrived "explanatory structure."[2] In the end, he concluded, every biography is actually autobiographical, but rather than revealing that fact to their reading audience, as true autobiographers do, they "can only get it wrong, can only lie, can only substitute their own story for the story of their announced subject." Such chicanery renders the medium "a bad game," dishonest for its practitioners and a waste of time for readers who would be better served by watching wrestling on television.[3]

Whether one agrees with Fish or not, he is right on one count. All biography is, in part, autobiographical. Few, if any, biographers would choose a subject if the themes of that life were not interesting enough to sustain research and writing over the course of years or even decades.[4] Thus, one can assume that some aspect of the theme explored resonates deeply within the author. As for the rest of his argument, Fish performed a service by challenging biographers to think more deeply about the value of their writing and the methods of their craft.

Fish's essay will not diminish the number of biographies written or discourage avid readers from looking for the newest title. As William McFeely noted, biography has always mattered, for all of us share a "basic human curiosity about our fellow humans."[5] The late Barbara Tuchman, best known for her Pulitzer Prize–winning *The Guns of August* (1962) and *Stilwell and the American Experience in China* (1971), advised historians to exploit this human interest by using a biographical approach in their writings. As a "prism of history," biography attracts and holds the reader's interest in the larger subject.[6]

If Tuchman saw biography as a tool of history, the Greek writer Plutarch, author of *Lives of the Noble Greeks and Romans*, most of which was written in the first two decades of the second century CE, saw biography as a study that revealed who humans are. History, by contrast, examined their deeds.[7] In any case, in his time and for centuries afterward, both history and biography centered on members of the elite or those who had achieved political, military, or intellectual fame. Nonetheless, Plutarch, like many since, responded to his subjects in personal terms. Noting that he had begun his studies for "the sake of others," he soon found the enterprise useful for himself, "the virtues of these great men serving me as a sort of looking-glass, in which I may see how to adjust and adorn my own life."[8] In that statement, he identified the strong interest humans have shown in extracting moral lessons from past lives.

Although many readers of biography still seek moral inspiration, the British author Lytton Strachey rescued modern biography from the didacticism into which it had fallen during the Victorian era. In works such as

Eminent Victorians (1918) and *Queen Victoria* (1921), he used Freudian concepts to identify the hidden drives behind individual acts.[9] Consequently, modern readers are now more likely to seek a deeper understanding of human motivation and behavior as opposed to lessons that inculcate virtue.

We also seek knowledge about the human condition. As men and women, we do not simply live out the life of our species. Instead, we display a wide variety of native abilities, and our personalities and characters are shaped by our consciousness of our race and gender, environmental influences such as the class we belong to, our early education, indoctrination, and the choices we make. Well-written biography gives us a study of how these factors operate in the life of another person, based on the assurance that what appears in the work will rely on "discovery, not invention," according to Ira Bruce Nadel.[10] The finished product represents the biographer's attempt, within this restriction, to interpret the subject's life so that the personality of that individual is evoked. When that happens, according to Frank E. Vandiver, "a living being walks off the pages."[11] Then we experience the immense and often addictive pleasure of living someone else's life, while we go about the business of leading our own in the here and now.

Everyone who writes biographies has been inspired by the work of those who have succeeded in explaining the dynamics of a personality and a subject's hidden motives so that "a living being walks off the pages." Among the works that have breathed life into a figure, for me, is Fawn Brodie's *Thomas Jefferson: An Intimate History*.[12] The work is psychobiography, a category that many historians and biographers alike regard with suspicion, and with good reason. Neither historians nor biographers are usually trained professionals in the behavioral sciences. Moreover, many of the psychological or psychoanalytical theories that psychobiographers have often invoked have been discredited or at the very least subjected to scathing criticism.[13]

But it was not Brodie's use of Erik Erickson's psychological theory that struck me most forcefully. Rather, although the women's movement of the 1960s had emphasized that "the personal is political," in the early 1970s that insight was applied largely to the female half of the population. Biographers of male figures described their upbringing and family life but only as part of environmental influences. They might describe, for example, the effect of a father on a male figure, but domestic issues and concerns belonged to women, who appeared in supporting roles and often received only brief mention. The idea of separate spheres for men and women had been articulated in the emerging field of women's history, but, more important, it was accepted as a given in biography as a whole. What Brodie did was apply the insight that "the personal is political" to an intellectual giant in American history—a true American *philosophe*. In the process, the sage of Monticello emerged from the pages of her book as a truly human figure for the first time.

Jefferson, as Brodie noted in her opening survey of historical opinion, was an elusive figure, despite his extensive writings. She was not deterred in her investigation into his character. By reexamining the evidence that other scholars had used and by searching for "feeling as well as fact, for nuance and metaphor as well as idea and action," she offered a new interpretation of his life story.[14] It was one that was based on "the *connections* between his public life and his inner life, as well as his intimate life."[15]

In describing Jefferson's reluctance to assume responsibility at critical points in his career, earlier writers had viewed Jefferson's withdrawals as an inexplicable flaw in his temperament or character. Brodie saw it differently. She noted, for example, that Jefferson's refusal to join the American delegation in France in 1776 stemmed, in all probability, from his wife's pregnancy. Since each successive pregnancy placed Martha Jefferson's life in jeopardy, he could not leave the country when she might die in childbirth. Brodie uncovered a similar situation, in which Jefferson resigned from the Virginia legislature in December 1781 and refused a seat in the Continental Congress. Again his wife was pregnant, and this time, after giving birth the following May, she never recovered, dying in September of that year. Jefferson's fears for her safety had been warranted, and his refusal to accept public responsibility had stemmed, Brodie surmised, from his concern with intimate family matters, an area that statesmen of his era seldom discussed publicly.[16]

Brodie's biography aroused controversy when she argued that, during his widowhood, Jefferson fathered children by his slave, Sally Hemings, his late wife's half-sister. Brodie based her claim on the narrative of

Madison Hemings (a son of Sally Hemings, who remembered Jefferson as an aloof father and master at Monticello), circumstantial evidence of the dates of Sally Hemings's pregnancies, and accounts from Jefferson's enemies. With DNA evidence indicating in 1998 that either Jefferson or a very close relative fathered at least one of Sally Hemings's children, Brodie's conclusions about their relationship have greater credence today than they did in 1974.[17] Moreover, even if Brodie was wrong about the Jefferson-Hemings relationship (and I doubt that she was), and one of Jefferson's relatives actually fathered Sally Hemings's children, a deeper truth emerges from her work. Many of the slaves on Southern plantations were family members, and they and their owners were bound together by ties of love, guilt, and denial.

Beyond that insight, Brodie was telling us that men, as well as women, make critical decisions in their lives on the basis of intimate or domestic concerns. Thus, attention to a man's private concerns could illuminate his public life in ways that standard political or military biographies of an earlier era had largely ignored. Although one would not turn to her biography for the best analysis of Jefferson's intellectual development and contributions to American political thought, or of his career as a party leader and president, one should not leave her out of those discussions. By considering the ties between the personal and the political and bringing them concretely into historical discussion, Brodie was a pioneering scholar who still deserves the gratitude of those who grapple with the task of writing biography.[18]

The value of Brodie's insight was revealed to me in the early 1980s. At that time, my husband, William Leckie, and I were examining the immense correspondence of Benjamin and Alice Kirk Grierson in the Illinois State Historical Library in preparation for writing a biography of the couple that would include their children. Grierson was a cavalry commander who led a diversionary raid through Mississippi during the Civil War while General Ulysses S. Grant was assaulting Vicksburg, and led an even more devastating raid through the state in 1864. Later, Grierson commanded the Tenth Cavalry—one of the units of "buffalo soldiers" in the post–Civil War frontier army. The deaths of three of seven children and the predisposition to manic-depressive psychosis of two surviving sons haunted him and Alice Grierson. Army life, which required frequent moves and often the separation of school-age children from parents, exacerbated this couple's ongoing difficulties. Thus, Benjamin Grierson's entire military career was marked by severe turmoil as he struggled to reconcile his family's emotional needs with their financial requirements. That element became for us not a side bar but a vital part of his life story. [19]

Although middle-class families, such as the Griersons, saw men and women as living and working in their "separate spheres," the lines blurred for this couple. We discovered that Alice Grierson often functioned as an informal, but very real, adjutant to her husband when he was away from various frontier posts. She not only sent him information regarding military matters but intervened on behalf of the buffalo soldiers. In her view, the soldiers were often unjustly confined to the guardhouse, and she wanted them released immediately. [20]

Besides turning to biography to learn from an informed scholar his or her interpretation of a person's life in all its aspects, both public and private, readers want to know how a subject confronted the existential issues and questions that all humans face. These include more than "Why am I here?" and "What does my life mean?" At crucial times in their lives, individuals define or redefine themselves when circumstances force them to make difficult choices or when they remain unable to extricate themselves from their past.

Louis Harlan, in his two-volume biography of Booker T. Washington, treated such issues in ways that are immensely instructive. [21] He gave his readers no simple answers but allowed the evidence to yield both insights and contradictions. In his interpretation, Washington, the last black leader born in slavery, grew up during Reconstruction and saw that African Americans could not protect their political rights in the South without an economic base. In his thirties, as he built Tuskegee, he split his public and private personas and became "willing to trade political independence for educational and economic gain." [22] Thus, Washington endorsed the idea that only the educated and propertied should vote, which was another way of saying that black men, most of whom were poor in the South, should avoid politics. His message comforted white Southern leaders, especially when he also advised members of his race to eschew the drive for social equality, thereby pledging black acceptance of segregation. That was, Harlan informed us, the point of his famous speech at the Atlanta Exposition of 1895, when he counseled blacks to accept a Faustian bargain as the price of peace. Simultaneously, he told Southern whites, wedded to the New South dream, and Northern capitalists, who sought lucrative investments in the region, that members of his race wanted their share of the hoped-for but never-realized prosperity as the price of their compliance with segregation.[23]

That said, Washington, as a black man, never took his own advice, despite his outward demeanor. Armed with contributions from industrialists and financiers, he began transforming Tuskegee Normal and Industrial Institute into the headquarters of his own political machine. At the same time, a product of his environment, he ran that school as if it were his own plantation.[24] A man of many masks, Washington had the intuitive ability to penetrate the facades of others. He played a variety of roles, depending on his objectives at any given time and the groups with which he interacted.

In the end, Harlan found that the "wizard" of Tuskegee used the power of his political machine surreptitiously—at times to maintain his power base, and at times to serve his people. To accomplish the first goal, he infiltrated the organizations of his rivals. To achieve the latter goal, he secretly financed suits against segregation in public facilities and against the grandfather clause, one of a number of methods that white authorities used in several states to prevent blacks from voting.[25] In that sense, the man who counseled accommodation also contributed to the emergence of the Civil Rights movement. It was, however, a movement that he never could have joined since it flourished in urban settings, and he remained throughout his entire, life the rural leader of a rural population.[26]

Nonetheless, Harlan's attention to the discrepancy between Washington's public persona and his private realities, as well as the wizard's way of exploiting the best of a bad situation to extract the maximum possible gain, left a deep impression on me that affected my thinking about Elizabeth Bacon Custer's widowhood. The death of her husband, George Armstrong Custer, was a severe blow, for she was left entirely alone in the world with no parents or siblings but only grieving in-laws who had lost three sons, a son-in-law, and a nephew at the Battle of the Little Bighorn in 1876.[27] And yet, in a very real sense, Elizabeth Custer's widowhood gave her a second life. Through her books—"Boots and Saddles"; or, Life in Dakota Territory with General Custer (1885); Tenting on the Plains; or, General Custer in Kansas and Texas (1887); and Following the Guidon (1890)—she transformed her imperfect husband into the model soldier and considerate comrade she wished he had always been. Her compatriots accepted her version because, as she understood so well, they needed a martyred rather than a discredited soldier as they wrestled with the complex moral problems of driving Indians from their land. At the same time, this woman, whose severest loss was that she never bore children, vicariously fulfilled her need to raise children by making her husband into a hero for boys.[28] Without in any way trivializing her sorrow over her husband's death and her fifty-seven years of widowhood and loneliness, the George Armstrong Custer that Elizabeth Custer resurrected in her books was closer to her desired ideal than the actual man. Consequently, by exploiting public sympathy and the predominant gender roles that made challenging her veracity an unchivalrous act, she reaped the benefits of being the widow of a hero and basked in the reflected glory she worked so hard to maintain.[29] It was a stunning achievement, but it came at a very high price: her ability to live a fully autonomous life. Still, just as Booker T. Washington never transcended his rural South of the Reconstruction era and its tragic aftermath, so Elizabeth Custer, a quintessential Victorian woman, never surmounted her view of herself as a family member first and an individual second.

I have learned from Brodie, who emphasized the importance of re-searching the private as well as public concerns of all individuals, and Harlan, who was willing to confront the discrepancy that often existed between public and private faces and the inability of some figures to transcend their larger environments. But other scholars have also affected my thinking about writing biography. In Writing Lives: Principia Biographica, a theoretical work, the late Leon Edel, best known for his five-volume work on Henry James, set down his thoughts on the medium and the pitfalls inherent in its practice.

The most difficult problem a biographer confronts, according to Edel, is dealing with himself. He has to be a "participant-observer," meaning that he has to play contradictory roles. As a participant, he must struggle to see the world as his subject saw it. At the same time, he must remain an "observer," for only then can he maintain the detachment needed to "distinguish between fact and fiction." This is important, for once the biographer crosses the line and incorporates fiction, "the enterprise is doomed."[30]

While maintaining this balance between empathy and detachment, the biographer must also explain the dynamics of the personality that emerges. Edel characterized this last as discovering "the shape under the rug," or the hidden myth of a life.[31] To demonstrate his meaning, he subjected Ernest Hemingway's life, among others, to a brief analysis. Hemingway presented himself as pugnacious and unemotional, especially with other men. Beneath the surface, Edel argued, he was the opposite, for "a manly man doesn't need to prove his masculinity every moment of the day." Edel concluded that Hemingway's life and art were masks that deflected attention from his true self-concept, which was based on his fears and insecurities.[32] The story of what lay behind those masks—"the shape under the rug"—was the true subject of Hemingway's life story. The same holds true for all life writing, Edel maintained, for "the biographer who writes the life of his subject's self-concept passes through a facade into the inner house of life."[33]

William McFeely's Pulitzer Prize–winning *Grant: A Biography* accomplished Edel's goal. On the surface, Ulysses S. Grant was modest, unassuming, and relaxed among common folk. McFeely, however, saw him as a man driven by an intense fear of falling back into the failure and obscurity that had characterized his earlier life, except for a brief period during the U.S.-Mexican War. During the Civil War, his willingness to wage total war and to endure the title "Butcher Grant" catapulted him into the prominence that made him a strong candidate for the White House. McFeely stated that Grant "had forced himself out of the world of ordinary people by the most murderous acts of will and had doomed himself to spend the rest of his life looking for approval for having done so." He wanted the presidency, for "he had heard those cheers and he could not do without them."[34]

Once he assumed the presidency, Grant gravitated toward members of the creditor and entrepreneurial classes as a way of distancing himself, McFeely maintained, from ordinary men. McFeely saw this tendency displayed during a crisis in 1874. With the nation in the throes of the worst depression it had yet experienced, Grant vetoed a bill to expand the currency. He thereby killed a measure that would have alleviated the suffering of farmers and laborers — many of whom had fought under him at places like Spotsylvania Court House or Cold Harbor — in favor of "a policy that brought still greater profit to the successful."[35] In doing so, Grant not only repudiated himself in terms of who he really was — a man who had failed repeatedly at business in his earlier life — but he demonstrated the fundamental weakness at the core of his presidency. He affiliated himself so completely with the entrepreneurial class that he turned a blind eye to the corruption that infiltrated almost every aspect of his administration.[36]

Nor did McFeely find that the Hero of Appomattox displayed presidential courage when it came to upholding the constitutional rights of black men and women in the South. Instead, as violence, especially the murderous events in Mississippi, increased, Grant, concerned about politics, could not bring himself to take the strong measures that were needed to ensure justice for newly enfranchised blacks. Thus, for all intents and purposes, McFeely found that Reconstruction, as a noble experiment designed to bring about a "new birth of freedom," had failed even before Grant left office.[37]

Subsequent biographers have offered less critical views of Grant, both as a commander and as a president. Brooks Simpson interpreted him as a figure who achieved "triumph over adversity" and who was not callous about wartime losses.[38] Jean Edward Smith pointed out that during postwar Reconstruction, Grant strove to win passage and ratification of the Fifteenth Amendment to extend voting rights to black men and, despite continuing white Southern intransigency, fought hard for passage of the Ku Klux Klan Act to curb white violence against African Americans. Smith blamed the U.S. Supreme Court rather than Grant for weakening federal protection of newly enfranchised blacks in the South.[39] These new interpretations are exactly what we expect, for the writing of biography, like the writing of history, is always an unfinished business. Nonetheless, whatever the persuasiveness of the new views about Grant, McFeely's work remains a riveting example of how one author sought to decipher the dynamics behind an often impenetrable personality.

Edel's counsel that biographers look for the shape beneath the rug played a role in my interpretation of Angie Debo, the Oklahoma historian who pioneered in ethnohistory. The hidden myth of her life, I became convinced, stemmed from her attachment to the "Oklahoma spirit." In Oklahoma, luck as well as hard work and fortitude played a role in the making and unmaking of fortunes. Some families, for example, acquired the better land in the various runs that opened Oklahoma Territory to non-Indian settlement beginning in 1889. Later, luck smiled on a fortunate few when they discovered oil on their property.[40] Nonetheless, adherence to the "Oklahoma spirit," as Debo's parents informed their children, demanded cheerful stoicism in the face of whatever fortune decreed.

Since the Debos farmed poor land, they eventually sold it to enter into a hardware business that quickly failed. Years later, they discovered that the new owners of their former homestead had located oil on the property. Debo told a friend that her father, Edward Debo, never expressed regret about selling his quarter section. Instead, whenever he passed the site, he recalled the good times they had enjoyed at their old home.[41] Edward Debo's message was clear: One never expressed anger or resentment over one's fate but instead rose above it.[42]

Later, when Angie Debo was dismissed from West Texas State Teachers College shortly after she injured her chairman's pride by becoming the first female faculty member in the college to earn her doctorate, she fell into despondency. She had no way of acknowledging her anger and resentment except by turning these emotions inward. But when she began investigating the fate of the Five Tribes of Oklahoma—the Cherokees, Choctaws, Chickasaws, Creeks, and Seminoles—following the termination of their separate republics and their tribal lands, she found her life's work. She could speak out on behalf of American Indians and the injustices they had experienced in a way that she could never have spoken out for herself. That channeling of unacceptable emotions into research, writing, and, later, activism on behalf of native peoples as they sought self-determination allowed Debo to sustain her own personal myth. In oral history interviews, she saw herself as a woman of equanimity who was free from anger and resentment, despite gender and class discrimination and years of poverty and professional marginalization.[43]

In addition to counseling the biographer to search for "the life of his subject's self-concept," Leon Edel also reminded biographers to place their subjects securely within the historical context of their times. Indeed, biography was a part of history and demanded "the same skills." But beyond that, no subject ever lived outside of human time and history. Therefore, Edel concluded, "No biography is complete unless it reveals the individual within history, within an ethos and a social complex."[44]

One author who has demonstrated his ability to weave biography and history together so that the two illuminate each other is Garry Wills. In *Reagan's America*, he narrated President Ronald Reagan's life. Simultaneously, based on his own painstaking research, Wills compared and contrasted the factual information with the often inaccurate passages in Reagan's autobiography, *Where's the Rest of Me?*[45] Throughout the Reagan biography, Wills also provided a larger historical context that contradicted much of Reagan's personal mythology. By including descriptions of army campaigns against native peoples, federal road-building projects, and governmental railroad subsidies, as well as New Deal programs that sustained the Reagan family during the Great Depression, Wills underscored the discrepancy between Reagan's version of the American past and the historical record. Ironically, the federal government that played such an important role in the larger historical context of Reagan's life was the same entity that Reagan castigated to achieve its highest office—the presidency of the United States.[46]

Toward the end of this remarkable work, Wills asks us, as readers, to think of ourselves as drivers who cannot see the road ahead when we try to use history as a means of discerning the future. "To steer at all, we must go forward looking into the rearview mirror, trying to trace large curves or bending forces in prior events, to proceed along their lines. But what happens if," he asks, "when we look into our historical rearview mirror, all we can see is a movie?"[47] His message was clear; Reagan's psychological needs and projections created a fiction of his own life and American history that he used to navigate the United States. More important, large numbers of Americans served as his "complicit" public.

Preferring comforting myth to troubling reality, they accepted his more optimistic version of the past and present, rather than engaging in the more strenuous activity of grappling with a host of difficult problems that had no easy solutions.[48]

My praise of Wills's work does not mean that his interpretation is unassailable. Reagan remains a contested figure. New biographies have praised him for restoring a sense of confidence to Americans during his presidency. Some credit him with bringing the Cold War to an end, an event that had not yet happened when Wills's book was originally published. The debate will go on and new interpretations will emerge, not only because new voices will enter the discussion, but also because these voices will have experienced the particular currents of their time. That, in turn, will affect their analyses and evaluations.[49]

The excellent biographies of the recent past and the increasing sophistication of many of biography's most able practitioners help account for the form's continuing popularity. Biography matters because we need it for inspiration, consolation, and companionship, which we derive when "a living being walks off the pages" and we feel that we actually know another human being more intimately than we know many of the individuals with whom we interact daily. At the same time, we also want to know how others have made the difficult choices that confront all of us as human beings and how they lived with the often-unintended consequences of those choices. We also value biography as a way of encountering the personal myths of others, so that we might reflect on our own personal mythmaking and perhaps achieve a deeper understanding of ourselves through others. Finally, we want to understand the extent to which history molds individuals and, in turn, is influenced by individuals. All these are popular and important reasons that biography matters to the general public and will continue to matter for the foreseeable future.

But there is another reason that biography matters today more than in the past, and it is because of its interrelationship with history. Scholar Gerda Lerner, like Wills, argued that history gives a sense of direction to life. In much of the world, she noted, religion, which passed from generation to generation in rural and agrarian societies, had traditionally served as the way people infused their lives with meaning. Now, however, many people have moved from rural areas to increasingly urbanized regions.[50] In that context, history matters more than ever. As Lerner reminded us, "In a world in which personal contact with different generations is often severed," history can "link people to past generations and root them in the continuity of the human enterprise."[51] Since our view of the future, moreover, is derived largely from our interpretation of the past, the prevailing beliefs about history affect the future and carry immense power. Those outside the academy understand that fact, which, Lerner observed, explains the "culture wars" of the 1980s and 1990s. More than ever, historians need to bridge the chasm that has opened between them and the public. For without historians' insights, the public will formulate its views on the basis of myth—or, as Wills noted, the movie that replaces the rearview mirror of history.[52]

History was never easy to write, but it is now a more complex and taxing enterprise than ever, and one fraught with new challenges. In part, this gulf between historians and the public has opened because many scholars, aware that their predecessors celebrated a Eurocentric and often ethnocentric view of the past, have struggled to weave into their narratives the stories of people of color and women as well as men. Moreover, they have sought to show race, gender, ethnicity, and class as social constructs, dependent upon time, place, and changing ideology. This new history demands more of its readers, making the historian's task of reaching the general public even harder than before.

The effect of these developments is obvious in the study of the American West. Historians who chronicle the entry of non-Indian people into the Trans-Mississippi West have witnessed an ongoing debate between adherents of the Old Western History and those of the New Western History. The former, still reflecting the attitudes, if not always the actual ideas, of Frederick Jackson Turner's 1893 essay "The Significance of the Frontier in American History," have interpreted their nation's past as the story of courageous settlers moving westward into free land to achieve freedom and economic and social mobility.[53] When the Bureau of the Census announced in 1890 that the frontier had closed, Turner warned that the United States now faced a turning point. No longer could the nation look to free land in the West as the solution to lack of opportunity and mobility in the East. The New Western Historians, by contrast, have argued that non-Indian movement into the American West represented conquest rather than settlement. Moreover, they have seen no broken past of the American West as a result of the Bureau of the Census's declaration that the frontier had closed in 1890 and the nation no longer had within its midst areas of unsettled land. Instead they argued that the problems that persist in the region often stemmed from the earlier period when Euro-Americans seized the land and its resources from native and Hispanic peoples. To make matters worse, they added, these newcomers to the West created a caste system that relegated people of color to inequality and sought to destroy their culture.[54]

The ideas of the New Western Historians have won widespread, although not universal, acceptance among academics. Certainly, their essays appeared frequently in academic journals. The general public, however, has preferred the Old Western History, which revolves largely around prospectors, cowboys, and cavalrymen. Wild West, a celebration of the traditional Turnerian story, still boasts sales that total more than 150,000 bimonthly. Old West and True West also enjoy large circulations. The Western Historical Quarterly, the foremost scholarly journal in the field, by contrast, prints about 2,500 copies of its periodical every three months.[55]

How do professional historians, especially those who wish to incorporate some of the insights of the New Western Historians into their work, bridge this gap and reach that larger audience? Clear and well-written revisionist history is one way of attacking this problem. Here Patricia Limerick has achieved a high standard of readability by using humor and self-disclosure and by having a wide-ranging knowledge and strong convictions.[56]

Another way of reaching a wider audience is to exploit the readers' strong interest in other people by writing biographies that tell the story of the American West from the perspective of individuals who belonged to groups that have been marginalized in the past. In other words, biographers need to tell the story from the perspective of those who stood on the other side of Turner's frontier. To succeed in their task, they must incorporate the more complicated context of current historical studies into their works. At the same time, they must write their works to the highest literary standards with a minimum of jargon so that they can engage the reader and win as wide an audience as possible.

Biographers who attempt to write the life story of individuals who come from groups that have been marginalized because of their race, gender, ethnicity, or class face problems that writers of more conventional biographies—those of "representative men"—do not confront. Sources are often lacking, especially for the subject's early years. When sources are available, intricate questions of interpretation often arise. Nonetheless, such problems can be surmounted. In the only biography that she wrote, Angie Debo indicated some ways in which to do this.

In 1976 the University of Oklahoma Press published Debo's *Geronimo: The Man, His Time, His Place*. Estimating the Chiricahua Apache's date of birth as about 1823 and finding little information on his childhood and upbringing, Debo narrated a probable account of his early years. She based it on the oral history interviews she had conducted with other Chiricahua; the published memoirs of Apache Jason Betzinez, a member of the closely related Mimbres band; and the writings of anthropologist Morris Opler, the foremost authority on the culture of the Apaches. When it came to the ongoing conflicts that affected Geronimo's life, Debo found the record more complete. For the most part the sources originated from Euro-American incursion into Apache land and U.S. government attempts to curb Apache raiding south of the U.S.-Mexican border, according to the terms of the 1848 Treaty of Guadalupe Hidalgo.

At a deeper level, Debo maintained, the conflicts arose because Geronimo and Euro-Americans, coming from different cultures, "never arrived at the same definition of truth." U.S. authorities and military leaders saw Geronimo as "a liar whose word could never be trusted." By bringing to bear the insights of the ethnologist, who understands that different cultures often assign different meanings to behavior, Debo discovered that, measured by his own standards, Geronimo was "a man of essential integrity." When he promised "with oath and ceremony—mere poetic trimmings to the white man—he kept his pledge."[57] The significance of his life story lay in the cultural divide that neither side was capable of bridging.

In 1992 historian Julie Roy Jeffrey published a work that delved into the subject of gender ideology as a factor in non-Indian penetration into the West, and its effect on native people. *Converting the West: A Biography of Narcissa Whitman* told the story of a female missionary from Auburn, New York. Influenced by the Second Great Awakening and thoroughly imbued with a sense of the superiority of middle-class family life and its prevailing gender roles, Narcissa Whitman worked with her husband, physician Marcus Whitman, in Oregon Territory in the late 1830s and 1840s, trying to bring Christianity to the Cayuse Indians. Her efforts to spread the gospel failed to convert a single member of that tribe, largely because she never transcended her ethnocentrism.[58] In 1847 the futility of her effort became apparent when the Cayuse murdered her and her family, following an outbreak of measles. That disease, which claimed the lives of many native people, left the missionaries and their children with few casualties.

Jeffrey's work is notable because, in the Turnerian school, Narcissa Whitman has been a celebrated figure. As one of the first white women to cross the North American continent in 1836 (Eliza Spalding was the other), she has long served as an icon of the westward movement. Jeffrey's biography, by presenting Narcissa Whitman as a woman thoroughly imbued with a sense of superiority, exposed the cultural arrogance that often persisted among non-Indian settlers in the West. This immensely readable and poignant work brings that message home to readers with an immediacy that will prove beneficial when they turn to the more difficult analytical works dealing with conflict and accommodation between and among Americanos and Hispanos (or the original Hispanic peoples, an admixture of Spanish, Mestizo, Pueblo, and nomadic Indian ancestry) and the migrants who moved northward from Mexico over succeeding decades.

Although the male icon of the West has been the cowboy in the image of John Wayne or Clint Eastwood, no region of the United States has been more ethnically diverse than the Trans-Mississippi West. Richard Griswold del Castillo and Richard A. Garcia's *César Chávez: A Triumph of Spirit* (1995) explored the life of a Mexican American, or Mexicano, who transformed his personal quest for acceptance into a larger struggle—the attainment of social justice for farm laborers who worked for a pittance in the western "factories in the field."[59]

Because Mexican Americans in the United States have faced intense discrimination, especially in a part of the West that had belonged to Mexico until 1848, Griswold del Castillo and Garcia have performed a valuable service for general readers and historians alike. The general reader can profit from a clearer understanding of the difficulties Mexican Americans have faced by viewing them through the engaging and moving prism of Chávez's life. Moreover, after reading this biography, that reader, very likely, will be more interested in learning about the larger context of U.S.-Mexican relations and the way that shifts in that relationship have affected Mexicans and Mexican Americans in the southwestern borderland.[60] This increased interest results because, in their prizewinning biography, the authors have brought César Chávez to life as the most prominent leader of his ethnic group in America and also as one who spoke for the rights of all working Americans.

Because the West is the part of our nation that has given us our origin myth, we need biographies of historians who have written about that area. The general public often views history as facts waiting to be discovered in a repository somewhere. Presumably, once historians find the facts and put them down on paper, the past will have yielded its secrets. Many have little understanding that both history and biography are the result of constant interpretation and reinterpretations based on new questions and concerns that arise in every decade and generation. Learning more about the life of historians would inform a wider audience of the true nature of historical inquiry and its value to their lives.

Some progress has been made in this area. In 1997 Allan Bogue published his magisterial *Frederick Jackson Turner: Strange Roads Going Down*, which shed light on Turner's world. Significantly, Turner came of age as the work of the historian was becoming professionalized through training in university seminars.[61] Although Bogue did not discuss at length the gendered nature of this process, it was obvious in Turner's relations with students such as Louise Kellogg. A protégée of the master, Kellogg spent her working life at the Wisconsin Historical Society, rather than teaching at the University of Wisconsin. In Turner's view, which was shared by his colleagues, academic jobs should go to men, rather than women.[62]

The work that explores more fully the tie between the writing of the history of the West and the importance of gender as a social construct that governed the opportunities for female scholars has not yet been written. When it is, the approach must be biographical. Even a cursory examination of the works of female historians such as Annie Heloise Abel, Angie Debo, and Mari Sandoz shows that they were far less wedded to the idea that non-Indians moved onto "free land." Instead, they realized that the land belonged to native people who called it their home. Moreover, when these women wrote about native peoples, they described them as agents and actors on the historical stage rather than mere foils for the white man's saga of conquest.[63]

Jacques Barzun and Henry F. Graff defined history as "vicarious experience." By this they meant that it gives individuals "a second life extended indefinitely into the 'dark backward and abysm of time.'"[64] Biography gives us instances of "vicarious experience." An author who succeeds in evoking a life gives us a precious gift that should not be discarded or denigrated as "minutiae without meaning."

At the same time, those of us who labor in the libraries and offices in which we write biographies must be humble about our abilities and mindful of our responsibilities. The biographies we produce are our works in the sense that no other person would have written the same life story of any one individual. If we have done our work well, our biographies will not be "definitive," in the sense of defining a person once and for all. Instead, our greatest accomplishment will be to present a portrait of that individual that will motivate others to conduct their own research into the existing evidence of the life that was lived. When those new biographies are written, all of us will be richer for the insights they will disclose.

"All biography," Leon Edel informed his readers, "is, in effect, a reprojection into words, into a literary or a kind of semiscientific and historical form, of the inert materials, reassembled, so to speak, through the mind of the historian or the biographer. His," Edel continued, "becomes the informing mind. He can only lay bare the facts as he has understood them, in a continuous and inquiring narrative." Without that "informing mind," the subject would enjoy, at best, only a flicker of afterlife. Edel quoted novelist Joseph Conrad's statement on this point: "The dead can live only with the exact intensity and quality of the life imparted to them by the living."[65] There is no other way, and that is why biography has always mattered.

Today, because professional historians need the biographers' life stories as a way of helping bridge the gap between themselves and a larger reading public, biography matters more than it mattered in the past. As our globe becomes smaller and our communities more diverse, biography, which breathes life into dry census data and puts faces on demographic tables, will become the means by which to weave the stories of new groups into our national fabric. In the "intensity and quality of the life imparted" lies our best hope for the revitalization of history as an academic discipline that will reach and engage the larger audience and bring to it the perspectives of those who, for far too long, have been relegated to history's margins.

Notes

1. Stanley Fish, "Just Published: Minutiae without Meaning," New York Times, 7 September 1999, Section A, p. 19.

2. Fish, "Minutiae without Meaning," p. 19.

3. Fish, "Minutiae without Meaning," p. 19.

4. For a discussion on this point, see Newell G. Bringhurst, Fawn Brodie: A Biographer's Life (Norman: University of Oklahoma Press, 1999), xiii–xiv.

5. William McFeely, "Why Biography?" in The Seductions of Biography, ed. Mary Rhiel and David Suchoff (New York: Routledge, 1996), xiii.

6. Barbara Tuchman, "Biography as a Prism of History," in Telling Lives: The Biographer's Art, ed. Marc Pachter (Washington DC: New Republic Books, 1979), 134.

7. Catherine N. Parke, Biography: Writing Lives (New York: Twayne, 1996), 6.

8. Plutarch's Lives of Illustrious Men, trans. John Dryden et al., 3 vols. (New York: John Wurtele Lovell, [1880?]), 1: 375. For a slightly different translation, see: Greek Lives: A Selection of Nine Lives, trans. Robin Waterfield (Oxford: Oxford University Press, 1998), xiii.

9. Lytton Strachey, Eminent Victorians (London: Chatto & Windus, 1918); Queen

Victoria (New York: Harcourt, Brace, 1921). For a discussion of Strachey's use of Freud, see Leon Edel, *Writing Lives: Principia Biographica* (New York: W. W. Norton, 1984), 84.

10. Ira Bruce Nadel, *Biography: Fiction, Fact, and Form* (New York: St. Martin's Press, 1984), 55.

11. Frank E. Vandiver, "Biography as an Agent of Humanism," *The Biographer's Gift: Life Histories and Humanism*, ed. James F. Veninga (College Station: Texas A&M University Press, 1983), 16.

12. Fawn M. Brodie, *Thomas Jefferson: An Intimate History* (New York: W. W. Norton, 1974).

13. See Cushing Strout, "The Uses and Abuses of Psychology in American History," *American Quarterly* 28 (1976): 324–42.

14. Brodie, *Thomas Jefferson*, 16.

15. Brodie, *Thomas Jefferson*, 15–25; quote, 25.

16. Brodie, *Thomas Jefferson*, 126–29, 162–68.

17. Brodie, *Thomas Jefferson*, 127–28, 229–33.

18. For excellent recent works on Jefferson, see Andrew Burstein, *The Inner Jefferson: Portrait of a Grieving Optimist* (Charlottesville: The University of Virginia Press, 1995), and Joseph J. Ellis, *American Sphinx: The Character of Thomas Jefferson* (New York: Alfred A. Knopf, 1996).

19. William H. Leckie and Shirley A. Leckie, *Unlikely Warriors: General Benjamin Grierson and His Family* (Norman: University of Oklahoma Press, 1984).

20. Leckie and Leckie, *Unlikely Warriors*, 155–56, 161–62. Linda Kerber, "Separate Spheres, Female Worlds, Woman's Place: The Rhetoric of Women's History," *Journal of American History* 75 (June 1988): 9–39, identified the idea of separate spheres as an imperfectly realized ideal that many women exploited to expand their power even within the public sphere.

21. Louis R. Harlan, *Booker T. Washington: The Making of a Black Leader, 1856–1901* (New York: Oxford University Press, 1972); Harlan, *Booker T. Washington: The Wizard of Tuskegee, 1901–1915* (New York: Oxford University Press, 1983).

22. Harlan, *Washington: Black Leader*, 157–75; quote, 158.

23. Harlan, *Washington: Black Leader*, 204–28.

24. Harlan, *Washington: Black Leader*, 254–87.

25. Harlan, *Washington: Black Leader*, 288–303.

26. Harlan, *Washington: Wizard*, 435–37.

27. Shirley A. Leckie, *Elizabeth Bacon Custer and the Making of a Myth* (Norman: University of Oklahoma Press, 1993), 191–206.

28. The first and third of Elizabeth Custer's books were published by Harpers & Bros.; Charles L. Webster published the second. One critic suggested that "*Boots and Saddles*" was suitable Sunday-school reading. Norman Fox, "Christianity and Manliness," review from untitled newspaper, 30 April 1885, "*Boots and Saddles*" Scrapbook of Reviews, Custer Collection, box 7, Monroe County (Michigan) Historical Commission Archives. More important, by 1901, Charles Scribner & Sons had condensed Custer's three books into *The Boy General*, a textbook that purported to teach children civic virtues, including "lessons in manliness that mean more than dates and statistics." See "Opinions of the Press on *The Boy General*," brochure issued by Scribner Series of School Reading, 1901, Brice C. W. Custer Collection (private collection, copy in author's personal collection). *The Boy General* was edited by Mary E. Burt.

29. Leckie, *Elizabeth Bacon Custer*, 195–313.

30. Edel, *Writing Lives*, 62–66.

31. Leon Edel, "The Figure under the Carpet," *Telling Lives*, ed. Marc Pachter (Washington DC: New Republic Books, 1979), 30. The essay in this work is a slightly revised version of the chapter "Myth" in Edel's *Writing Lives*, 159–73.

32. Edel, "Figure under the Carpet," 27.

33. Edel, "Figure under the Carpet," 32.

34. William S. McFeely, *Grant: A Biography* (New York: W. W. Norton, 1981), xiii, 2. For information on Grant's military career after he became lieutenant general of the Union army, see 152–215.

35. McFeely, *Grant: A Biography*, 396–67.

36. McFeely, *Grant: A Biography*, 319–99.

37. McFeely, *Grant: A Biography*, 416–25.

38. Brooks Simpson, *Ulysses S. Grant: Triumph over Adversity, 1822–1865* (Boston: Houghton Mifflin, 2000), 416–25.

39. Jean Edward Smith, *Grant* (New York: Simon & Schuster, 2001), 542–72.

40. I am indebted to essays in *The Culture of Oklahoma*, ed. Howard F. Stein and Robert F. Hill (Norman: University of Oklahoma Press, 1993). Among those that most influenced my perception of Oklahoma attitudes are Howard Lamar, "The Creation of Oklahoma: New Meanings for the Oklahoma Land Run," 29–47; J. Neil Henderson, "Spa in the Dust Bowl: Oklahoma's Hidden Paradise," 131–42; and Pat Bellmon, "The Passing of Grit: Observations of a Farm Girl, Now a Spectator on the Land," 186–97.

41. Sara Doyle to Angie Debo, 28 March 1958, Angie Debo Papers [hereafter

ADP], Manuscript Collections, Edmon Low Library, Oklahoma State University, Stillwater, Oklahoma.

42. Angie Debo, "The Debos," unpublished family history, ADP; typescript of interviews conducted with Angie Debo by Glenna Matthew, Gloria Valencia Weber, and Aletha Rogers, 11 November 1984, p. 1, ADP.

43. See Shirley A. Leckie, *Angie Debo: Pioneering Historian* (Norman: University of Oklahoma Press, 2000), esp. 43, 71–83, 89, 178–86.

44. Edel, *Writing Lives*, 4.

45. Garry Wills, *Reagan's America* (New York: Penguin Books, 1988). See 36, 41, 58–60, 70, 74, 82–85, 103, 143, 149, 199–203, 263, 267, 280–4, 295–96, 324–31, 339–43. For Reagan's statements about his life, Wills quotes extensively from Ronald Regan, *Where's the Rest of Me?* With Richard G. Hubler (New York: Duell, Sloan & Pearce, 1965).

46. Wills, *Reagan's America*, 93–111, 332–43.

47. Wills, *Reagan's America*, 460.

48. Wills, *Reagan's America*, 466–67.

49. *Reagan's America* was published in 1987 under the title *Innocents at Home: Reagan's America*, which emphasized the naïveté of the American public, but it was changed with the 1988 Penguin edition. For a recent biography that is fairly balanced, see William E. Pemberton, *Exit with Honor: The Life and Presidency of Ronald Reagan* (Armonk NY: M. E. Sharpe, 1997).

50. Gerda Lerner, *Why History Matters: Life and Thought* (New York: Oxford University Press, 1997), 200.

51. Lerner, *Why History Matters*, 200.

52. As renowned scholars gathered at the Wellesley College forum, "The Future of History," in April 2000, they heard warnings of a discipline that "is in danger of becoming too fragmented to be meaningful to students and too obscure to have much impact outside academe," according to Elizabeth Greene, "Plotting a Future for History," *Chronicle of Higher Education*, 28 April 2000, Section A, 18. See also David Oshinsky, "The Humpty Dumpty of Scholarship," *New York Times*, 26 August 2000, Section A, 17, 19.

53. Frederick Jackson Turner, "The Significance of the Frontier in American History," in *Frontier and Section: Selected Essays of Frederick Jackson Turner*, ed. Ray Allen Billington (Englewood Cliffs NJ: Prentice-Hall, 1961), 37–62. According to Lerner, *Why History Matters*, 202, the narrative of American History, as traditionally taught in schools and colleges, "used the doctrines of American exceptionalism

and Manifest Destiny and the myth of the triumphant conquest of the West as a legitimizing explanatory system."

54. Patricia Limerick, *The Legacy of Conquest: The Unbroken Past of the American West* (New York: W. W. Norton, 1987), 18, emphasized continuity, stating that "the conquest of Western America shapes the present as dramatically—and sometimes as perilously—as the old mines shape the mountainsides."

55. Richard W. Etulain, *Telling Western Stories: From Buffalo Bill to Larry McMurtry* (Albuquerque: University of New Mexico Press, 1999), 151–52.

56. Patricia Limerick, *Something in the Soil: Legacies and Reckonings in the New West* (New York: W. W. Norton, 2000), 333–43.

57. Angie Debo, *Geronimo: The Man, His Time, His Place* (Norman: University of Oklahoma Press, 1976), xi.

58. Julie Roy Jeffrey, *Converting the West: A Biography of Narcissa Whitman* (Norman: University of Oklahoma Press, 1991).

59. Richard Griswold del Castillo and Richard A. Garcia, *César Chávez: A Triumph of Spirit* (Norman: University of Oklahoma Press, 1995). Carey McWilliams, "The Mexican Problem," *Common Ground* 8 (spring 1948): 3–17, coined the phrase "factories in the field."

60. David G. Gutiérrez, *Walls and Mirrors: Mexican Americans, Mexican Immigrants, and the Politics of Ethnicity* (Berkeley and Los Angeles: University of California Press, 1995), another prizewinning work, achieved a very high level of scholarship, but many sections are theoretical as the author analyzes arguments about legal issues and debates over affirmative action. Thus it presupposes a depth of understanding on the reader's part that is usually lacking in a popular audience. However, were I teaching a course on ethnic minorities in the southwestern United States, I would assign *César Chávez: A Triumph of Spirit* to my students, and once we had discussed the issues raised in this work, I could then assign *Walls and Mirrors*. The clearly written and moving biography would have elicited student interest, and, even more important, a measure of student empathy for the situation Mexicanos and Mexicanas have faced in the U.S. borderlands of the Southwest.

61. Allan Bogue, *Frederick Jackson Turner: Strange Roads Going Down* (Norman: University of Oklahoma Press, 1997).

62. Bogue, *Strange Roads*, 123.

63. See, for example, Annie Eloise Abel, *The American Indian as Slaveholder and Secessionist* (Cleveland: A. H. Clark, 1915); Angie Debo, *And Still the Waters Run* (Princeton: Princeton University Press, 1940); Mari Sandoz, *Crazy Horse: The Strange Man of the Oglalas: A Biography* (Lincoln: University of Nebraska Press, 1942).

64. Jacques Barzun and Henry F. Graff, *The Modern Researcher*, 5th ed. (Fort Worth: Harcourt Brace Jovanovich, 1992), 40.

65. Edel, *Writing Lives*, 43.

Selected Bibliography

Bogue, Allan. *Frederick Jackson Turner: Strange Roads Going Down*. Norman: University of Oklahoma Press, 1997.

Bringhurst, Newell G. *Fawn Brodie: A Biographer's Life*. Norman: University of Oklahoma Press, 1999.

Brodie, Fawn M. *Thomas Jefferson: An Intimate History*. New York: W. W. Norton, 1974.

Debo, Angie. *Geronimo: The Man, His Time, His Place*. Norman: University of Oklahoma Press, 1976.

Edel, Leon. *Writing Lives: Principia Biographica*. New York: W. W. Norton, 1984.

Etulain, Richard W. *Telling Western Stories: From Buffalo Bill to Larry McMurtry*. Albuquerque: University of New Mexico Press, 1999.

Griswold del Castillo, Richard, and Richard A. Garcia. *César Chávez: A Triumph of Spirit*. Norman: University of Oklahoma Press, 1995.

Harlan, Louis R. *Booker T. Washington: The Making of a Black Leader, 1856–1901*. New York: Oxford University Press, 1972.

————. *Booker T. Washington: The Wizard of Tuskegee, 1901–1915*. New York: Oxford University Press, 1983.

Hood, Edwin Paxton. *The Uses of Biography, Romantic, Philosophic, and Didactic*. London: Partridge and Oakey, 1852.

Jeffrey, Julie Roy. *Converting the West: A Biography of Narcissa Whitman*. Norman: University of Oklahoma Press, 1991.

Lerner, Gerda. *Why History Matters: Life and Thought*. New York: Oxford University Press, 1997.

Limerick, Patricia N. *The Legacy of Conquest: The Unbroken Past of the American West*. New York: W. W. Norton, 1987.

McFeely, William S. *Grant: A Biography*. New York: W. W. Norton, 1981.

Nadel, Ira Bruce. *Biography: Fiction, Fact, and Form*. New York: St. Martin's Press, 1984.

Pachter, Marc, ed. *Telling Lives: The Biographer's Art*. Washington DC: New Republic Books, 1979.

Parke, Catherine N. *Biography: Writing Lives*. New York: Twayne, 1996.

Plutarch. *Plutarch's Lives of Illustrious Men.* Translated by John Dryden et al. 3 vols. New York: John Wurtele Lovell, 1880?

Rhiel, Mary, and David Suchoff. *The Seductions of Biography.* New York: Routledge, 1996.

Strachey, Lytton. *Eminent Victorians.* London: Chatto & Windus, 1918.

————. *Queen Victoria.* New York: Harcourt, Brace, 1921.

Veninga, James F., ed. *The Biographer's Gift: Life Histories and Humanism.* College Station: Texas A&M University Press, 1983.

Wills, Garry. *Reagan's America.* New York: Penguin Books, 1988.

2. Culture and Context in Biographical Studies: The Case of China

R. Keith Schoppa

Robert Rosenstone, observing the essential relationship between historians and the past as they interpret it, concluded that "History does not exist until it is created. And we create it in terms of our underlying values. Our kind of vigorous, 'scientific' history is in fact a product of our history, our special history that includes a particular relationship to the written word, a rationalized economy, notions of individual rights, and the nation-state. Many cultures have done quite well without this sort of history, which is only to say that there are—as we all know but rarely acknowledge—many ways to represent and relate to the past."[1]

Perhaps the most telling clause in Rosenstone's historiographical reflections is the parenthetical "as we all know but rarely acknowledge." Historians and biographers-as-historians are rooted in their particular cultures and contexts. Their created histories—in subject matter, approach, interpretation, methods, nuance—will reflect to some degree or other the culture and context that constitute their "special history." But, as in most endeavors, people rooted in a particular culture take that culture and its values as the norm and often quite unthinkingly assume its universal applicability. In his presidential address to the American Historical Association more than thirty years ago, noted China specialist John K. Fairbank argued that "historians in America have been, like historians elsewhere, patriotic, genetically oriented, and culture-bound."[2]

How do we see this American culture-boundedness in biographies? One of the four elements of American culture noted by Rosenstone, individualism, is at the center of our public ethos. Biography as a genre of historical writing obviously is congruent with that ethos. In the modern West, with its glorification of the individual, a biographer usually focuses on his or her subject's individuality, those aspects, attitudes, and abilities that separate the subject from the masses. Thus, in Nell Irvin Painter's masterful biography of Sojourner Truth, we find, among others, the following listings in the index under Truth: "anger of," "anxiety of," "canniness of," "clothing of," "drinking of," "guilt of," "humor of," "magnetism of," "public speaking of," "sexuality of," and "vulnerabilities of."[3] In other words, Painter strove to let us know who Truth was as an individual. Note one other point. The listings detailing anger, anxiety, guilt, sexuality, and vulnerabilities suggest that Painter intended to open Truth's psyche as well as can be done long after her death. Modern Western biographers often probe for explanations for life decisions and developments in the individual himself or herself by exploring the subject's psyche. Indeed, based upon the centrality of the individual and the importance of such concepts as individual fulfillment and self-realization, it can be said that psychology is the social/behavioral science *par excellence* in the modern West.

In the last several decades biographers have, to some degree or other, used psychological insights and explanations to shed light on their subjects. In a 1981 forum on the "new history" published in the *Journal of Interdisciplinary History*, Miles Shore wrote that the "highest expression of the biographer's art lies in the elucidation of the nuances of motivation and relationship that form the personal myth and make it possible to see the psychological unity within which action takes on meaning."[4] In the *American Historical Review*, Thomas Kohut argued more categorically that the psychological dimension "remains a historical subject of decisive importance. . . . Because it is not possible to comprehend people without dealing with the psychological, historians . . . have always written about it, even if they have rarely acknowledged the fact."[5]

As they stand, the statements by Shore and Kohut are blanket generalizations. Shore would likely argue that his stipulation about the "highest expression of the biographer's art" applies to any biographer and to any biographical subject; so too with Kohut's claim of the "decisive importance" of the psychological dimension. In their presentations, both scholars seem oblivious to the substance of Rosenstone's caution that there are "many ways to represent and relate to the past." Their pronouncements may indeed be appropriate for Western cultures. But can they apply to subjects in non-Western cultures in which values, customs, outlook, and priorities are drastically different?

As a measure of the chasm between Western and Eastern cultures, for example, take the meaning of the word "sincerity." Shore and Kohut would know what the word means in the West, as it fits neatly with their emphasis on psychology—"being true to one's inner feelings." But in traditional East Asian cultures it has had a strikingly different meaning, which represents a different social reality from that of the West. Sincerity in East Asia was "being true to one's social role." Thus, willingly marrying the fiancé to whom a woman's parents betrothed her when she was still a child was an act of "sincerity," the proper fulfillment of the social role of a daughter and woman. In feudal Japan a warrior-vassal committing ritual suicide (*seppuku*) at the behest of his lord showed "sincerity," dramatically underscoring his social relationship with the lord. The crucial social feature here is one's relationship to others. Sociology, not psychology, would be the social science par excellence in East Asia.

This West/East, psychology/sociology difference is, not surprisingly, reflected in the perceived reasons that people in these two broad cultural arenas have for reading biographies. In a review published in the *New York Review of Books*, Robert Darnton stated that "Biography . . . by focusing on one life . . . eliminates the complications that weigh down accounts of entire societies, and it adheres to a narrative line that shows individuals in action. It restores agency to history, giving readers a sense of closeness to the men and women who shaped events. It deals with motivations and emotions. It even answers a voyeuristic desire to see through keyholes and into private lives."[6]

Contrast this view with that of a 1995 piece in the *Beijing Review*, the semiofficial English-language periodical from the People's Republic of China: "Many biographies are of considerable historical value, presenting an important way to understand political figures and political life. The wide attention to such works indicates the public's interest in China's destiny and future, as well as their growing awareness of governmental and political affairs. . . . However[, the trend of writing about leaders as ordinary human beings] has produced some works that overemphasize trivialities to the neglect of significant historical events. Readers are becoming bored by such works, with sales drastically declining."[7]

Darnton emphasized the psychological and emotional attraction of biographies for Western readers. First of all, they simplify history, "eliminat[ing] the complications that weigh down accounts of entire societies." They "restore agency to history." Is this important for understanding the past? No, its main thrust (at least as it is described here) is to give readers a "sense of closeness" to biographical subjects. Heralding the psychological dimension that attracts readers to biographies, Darnton noted their inclusion of motivations, emotions, and lives behind closed doors. The *Beijing Review* article, in contrast, argued that the appeal of biographies to a Chinese readership stemmed from people's interest in current issues in China's modernizing polity. Nothing about enhancing the "closeness" of the reader and the biographical subject appeared here: Biographies are didactic, giving people information to help them understand contemporary developments. The piece positively frowns on probing the individuality of the subject, on the kind of personal, even voyeuristic appeal of biographies for "bourgeois" Westerners, noting that the declining sales of Chinese biographies emphasizing such "trivialities" indicated a bored reading public.

The crucial question that any biographer must answer is this: What is the most appropriate way to deal with the biographical subject so as to express in the most meaningful and coherent way the salient aspects of his or her life within its own cultural context? Vast differences in social values, priorities, and contexts, underscored by the ascribed diverse appeals of biographies in China and the United States, suggest that biographers dealing with subjects in cultures different from their own may need to ask different questions, have different emphases and priorities, and perhaps use different approaches. In this chapter, I will argue that this is indeed the case.

It is a commonplace to say that while the basic social unit in the modern West is the individual, in China it is the group. But the social reality is much deeper than is apparent in this simple generalization. It is when one is asked to describe the group in each society that one comes to see that there is a fundamentally different definition for *both* the individual and the group in these two cultures. For while in the modern West it is accurate to say that—other than in the family—individuals precede the group, in China the group precedes the individual. Put another way, in the West individuals make up a group; in China a group is composed of individuals. Because in the West individuals "make up" a group, they can also, as independent actors, freely make demands on the group or even leave the group. In China, because the group has precedence over its individuals, maintaining the group and its harmony is of primary concern. The group constrains individuals, for they cannot make claims of individual "rights" within the group without threatening the group's unity and cohesion. In this sense, the individual in traditional Chinese society was a much less "independent" actor than an individual in Western society. Contemporary poet Bei Dao ends his "Notes from the City of the Sun" with the line "Living, *A net.*"

A Chinese individual is constrained by groups and his or her relationships within groups as if he or she were linked to others by invisible threads that tied them all into a net. As in the West, individuals can leave the group, but in the process they will tear or break the net, and social and personal damage can be severe. Thus, in approaching a Chinese individual as a biographical subject, one must focus much attention not simply on the individual but on those people in the various groups that hold him or her in their nets. While the biography of a Westerner might likely consider people who play a large role in the subject's life or who help provide context and support, their presence would not likely loom so large because of the difference in the Western understanding of the greater autonomy or degree of "separateness" of the individual. Thus Nell Irvin Painter described the "networks" of Truth's antislavery feminism, but they seem to have existed primarily for her individual benefit; Painter told us that "those networks sustained her materially and spiritually, steadily broadening her horizons."[8] By contrast, in China networks tended to be constraining rather than liberating.

What kinds of relationships within groups create the particular dynamics of Chinese society on which a biographer must focus? Basic social identity comes not only from one's family and his or her place in it but from social connections and the networks that develop from them. An American journalist has written that the Chinese "instinctively divide people into those with whom they already have a fixed relationship, a connection, what the Chinese call *guanxi*, and those with whom they do not. These connections operate like a series of invisible threads, tying Chinese to each other with far greater tensile strength than mere friendship."[9] Connections and their logical next step, networks, were established in various ways.

Some relationships were certain to bring "connections." Friends obviously had close connections; the only one of the five Confucian bonds that was a bond suggesting equality rather than hierarchy was friendship. Certainly, for this reason friendship was more celebrated in Chinese literature than any other social relationship. If a person came from the same hometown or county or even province (in Chinese, "native place"), he or she would have a built-in connection with everyone else from that place. The connection was stronger further down the hierarchy of place—county or town or village, for example. Academic and scholarly ties were also significant sources of connections. The men who received civil service degrees in the same year shared a type of alumnus connection. Teacher-student relationships endured throughout life, taking on an almost master-disciple dynamic.

Certainly social connections are important in every culture, and any biography must consider them. But Chinese culture has, it seems to me, developed connections to the nth degree. They are immensely practical social realities. From the bureaucracy of the traditional state to that of the Communist state to that of the post-Communist state, people have used their personal social connections to get what they want or need. The person who uses connections to gain certain ends expends social capital and builds up social debts to the dispenser of favors or the facilitator of actions. Repaying those debts through reciprocal actions further nurtures the connection, making its "tensile strength" very great indeed. The accumulation and repaying of obligations is a continual social reality that a skillful biographer must take into consideration.

China's most famous twentieth-century sociologist, Fei Xiaotong, has written about the importance of connections and networks in the fundamental structure and processes of Chinese society. Networks may include many people, but it is important to note that their structure is dyadic, based on the connections between two people, and then two others, and so on. The strength of any two connections varies. Similarly, individuals may find themselves a part of a number of networks. The strength of the personal connections to people in each network also varies. This situation has definite ethical implications. Noting that Chinese society is structured as "webs woven out of countless personal relationships," Fei argued that "to each knot in these webs is attached a specific ethical principle." In this society, "general [ethical] standards have no utility. The first thing to do is to understand the specific context: Who is the important figure, and what kind of relationship is appropriate with that figure? Only then can one decide the ethical standards to be applied in that context."[10] Thus, there is no universal ethic to be applied to all people and in all situations. Ethics in China were traditionally determined by connections; they varied with particular people and situations. The biographer of a Chinese subject must be aware of this reality while interpreting the actions of that person.

These kinds of social realities and relativities gave Chinese social life considerable fluidity, in many or perhaps most cases providing a considerable challenge for the biographer. A person's social identity and place in society largely depended on those to whom he or she was connected. In the end, if someone with whom a person had spent years establishing and cultivating connections was kicked out of power, lost a job, was incapacitated, or died, then he or she was back to square one in trying to establish his or her own social position. Developing and nurturing personal connections was understandably a full-time, lifelong undertaking.

Thus, though I, as a modern Western biographer of an early twentieth-century Chinese man named Shen Dingyi, was interested in the individuality of my subject, my primary focus necessarily had to be on questions of social relationships. In the fluidity that was and is Chinese society, the biographer must be continually concerned about context, because the subject is embedded in different social networks in various arenas of life and action. One must analyze as carefully as possible the sources of individual connections and attempt to judge the relative strengths of connections between the subject and those with whom he or she had *guanxi*. This requires an awareness of the various networks of which the subject was a part, of the strength of each network in its effect on the subject, and of social dynamics within the networks. One must be aware that the subject likely played different roles in each connection and network, and that these different roles gave different identities. The biographer of a Chinese subject must not assume that the modern Western conception of human development—with stages of infancy, toddlerhood, childhood, adolescence, early adulthood, middle age, and old age—applies to Chinese. This cautionary note should be fairly obvious since studies of earlier times in the West have shown, for example, that during the Middle Ages there was no sense that childhood was a separate stage of life. It was not until the nineteenth century that adolescence came to be seen as a separate stage.[11] Professor Kenneth Keniston has argued that "In other societies or historical eras, puberty is . . . not followed by anything like what we consider an adolescent experience. . . . If, therefore, a given stage of life or development change is not recognized in a given society, we should seriously entertain the possibility that it simply does not occur in that society. And, if this is the case, then in societies where adolescence does not occur, many of the psychological characteristics which we consider the results of adolescent experience should be extremely rare: For example, a high degree of emancipation from family, a well-developed self-identity, a belief system based upon a reexamination of the cultural assumptions learned in childhood."[12]

China was one culture that did not have a conception of adolescence as a separate life stage. In Confucianism "adulthood" was thought to be made up of three "equally significant periods of human life" or three "integral aspects" or three "inseparable dimensions"—youth, manhood, and old age. "Maturation is perceived mainly in terms of self-cultivation"; adulthood thus is a "process of becoming," a "process of realizing that which is thought to be the authentic human nature." Though there is a difference between youth and manhood, there was no sense of a " 'between' period, alleged to be characterized by mental and emotional instability as well as other ingratiating attributes."[13] In Book 2 of the *Analects*, Confucius reportedly described the ages of man:

> At fifteen I set my heart on learning.
> At thirty I was firmly established.
> At forty I had no more doubts.
> At fifty I knew the will of Heaven.
> At sixty I was ready to listen to it.
> At seventy I could follow my heart without transgressing what
>   was right.[14]

Indeed, Western psychological theories and insights would be hard pressed to make any sort of appropriate contribution toward understanding a Chinese subject without a sense of adolescence and a concept of discrete stages of life.

Yet another cultural constraint on writing a biography of a Chinese person is the nature of the sources. Chinese sources detail those things that Chinese would see as important and significant. Since biographical sources were expected to provide records of public accomplishments to serve as a memorial to the subject and grist for didactic accounts, available sources provided the public "facts" of one's life "and such ideas as have been preserved in his published essays, memorials, and poetry. There [was] precious little else."[15]

Those sources that do exist have been shaped by Chinese cultural interests and values. Thus, the father-son relationship is frequently talked about and reflected upon; it was the prime Confucian social bond. Yet I have never seen mother-son relationships discussed. Nor were husband-wife relationships described. We may learn how many wives and concubines a man had, but we generally know nothing about the nature and dynamics of relationships between (among) them. Fei Xiaotong, in his description of rural society, reported that husbands and wives generally had little to do with each other socially, seeking same-sex companionship instead. Men and women were often betrothed in childhood, a practice indicating that childhood was not seen as a discrete stage from early adulthood. The couple often did not see each other until the day of their wedding. Upon marrying, a woman would leave her natal home for her husband's home. There she was in an inferior position not only to her husband but to her father-in-law and, most notoriously, to her mother-in-law. In the traditionally patriarchal society, females—whether wives, concubines, sisters, or lovers—were mostly invisible. Thus, the relationships that in the West would be standard fare and perhaps pivotal in biographies—mother-son, mother-father-son, husband-wife, lover-lover—were not generally noted or recorded.

Certainly the public record and facts of the life of Shen Dingyi provided some information about his individuality. We know that at age forty he left his wife and began to live with a much younger woman. From his memorial biography, meant to elevate him in the eyes of his peers, we learn that into his late thirties he was a heavy drinker. The biography stresses his decision to abandon this habit. From his relationships with others we can glean aspects of his personality and make circumstantial conclusions about his individuality. But traditional sources were not rich in insights into personality or individual idiosyncracies. In the 1980s and 1990s, however, a new type of source emerged in the People's Republic of China. Called wenshi ziliao (historical materials), these were compilations of various materials, ranging from accounts of historical events and developments, to personal memoirs, to biographies. The latter, more informal than traditional biographies, often give greater insight into the subject's individuality. The downside of these sources is that there is no quality control, so errors and biases abound. The biographer may use them at his or her own professional peril.

Shen Dingyi was what might be called a "second-tier" Chinese leader in the 1910s and 1920s. He came from a wealthy landlord family in Zhejiang, a central coastal province south of Shanghai. His father, who held several lower-level official positions, bought the twenty-one-year-old Shen the magistracy of a county in distant Yunnan Province. Shen, however, shamed his father and family by becoming involved in revolutionary activity, and in the end simply abandoning his post and fleeing to Japan. He spent substantial sums of his family's money to help bankroll the 1911

Chinese revolution that overthrew the Manchu Qing dynasty. Returning to China after the revolution as a political leader in Hangzhou, the provincial capital, Shen chaired the provincial assembly and emerged as chief spokesman during several provincial government crises in the late 1910s. Throughout his career he was impulsive and outspoken, an individualistic knight-errant who made fast friends and just as easily made bitter enemies.

Shen went to Shanghai in 1918 at the time of the cultural revolution that would become known as the May Fourth Movement—a campaign to purge China of traditional culture (in a slogan of the time, "Down with Confucius and sons") and to begin to structure a modern Chinese culture. There he coedited a progressive journal, *Weekly Review*, and wrote essays and poetry that espoused nationalism, socialism, feminism, and the transcendent importance of education. He became involved with a Marxist study group and became a member of the Shanghai Marxist cell that was a forerunner of the Chinese Communist party.

In 1920 Shen returned to his home village of Yaqian where he organized a free public school for the villagers. To teach there, he brought progressive, idealistic students with whom he had become acquainted. In 1921, reacting to the requests of several farmers, he took the initiative in organizing a farmers' rent-resistance movement. Although he was still a member of the provincial assembly and had come from a landlord background, Shen helped organize tenant farmers to strike against landlords. By the fall of 1921, "farmers' associations" had been established in eighty-two towns and villages in three counties with an estimated hundred thousand farmers and their families involved. The formation of an Alliance of Farmers' Associations at Yaqian finally mobilized landlords. Using their ties to the political and military establishments, they were able to arrange for the military in the area to crush the movement in mid-December. Leaders of the farm organization were jailed. Shen escaped reprisals, but he lost tremendous political capital and raised doubts and suspicions in many circles about his motives in the affair.

The Chinese Communist party was established in July 1921. In the early 1920s Soviet agents contacted Sun Yat-sen, the best-known Chinese revolutionary leader of the early twentieth century, offering to help restructure his party, the Guomindang (or, Nationalist party) and to set up a military academy to train a party army. Sun accepted, also making the decision that individual Communist party members could join the revamped Guomindang. Shen became a member of both parties. The goal of the parties, joined in a "united front," was twofold: first, to undertake a military campaign to unite China and wipe out the plague of warlords, who had fought each other for territory and control of China since 1916; and second, to drive out the imperialist powers, whose presence had continued to grow. For the two parties, the mid-1920s were spent preparing for revolution. In 1924 a series of minor irritants began to drive a wedge between Shen and more radical members of the provincial Guomindang, which was led at this time by the young teachers whom Shen had brought to teach at the Yaqian Village School. Sun Yat-sen's death in March 1925 unleashed party factionalism, which Sun had held in check until then. By the summer of 1925 the party had erupted into open, strident feuding between conservatives and radicals. This bitter party factionalism was exacerbated by the upsurge in nationalism following the British killings of Chinese demonstrators in Shanghai on 30 May. It was clear that the time for a revolutionary military campaign was nearing. Revolutionary choices—frequently the source of party factionalism—could no longer be postponed. In August, when a left-wing leader of the Guomindang was assassinated, the right wing was implicated.

In November 1925 Shen met with right-wing members before Sun Yatsen's coffin in the Western Hills near Beijing. Their purpose was to call for the ouster of all Communist party members who had joined the Guomindang, in effect halting the united front that had linked the parties, and for the expulsion of the chief Soviet adviser in China, Michael Borodin, who, they believed, had become too powerful. This meeting of what became known as the Western Hills faction openly split the Guomindang. In early 1926 both factions held their own party congresses. Shen was bitterly attacked by former colleagues who were active on the left in the province; the Western Hills faction was quickly tagged as far to the right or reactionary.

In the summer of 1926, the military campaign to unite the country, known as the Northern Expedition, got under way. Its military commander was Chiang Kai-shek, first associated with neither Right nor Left, but gradually moving into the rightist camp, though not so far right as the Western Hills group. Chiang and the National Army were successful in reaching the main Yangzi cities by the spring of 1927, when they struck out at the Guomindang Left and the Communists in bloody purges. The so-called White Terror, which lasted into 1928, temporarily ended all Communist party power. Shen emerged in Zhejiang Province in the summer of 1927 as head of purge activities and in the fall (October to December) as one of the provincial government leaders when circumstances brought Western Hills partisans to leadership in a number of provinces.

Ousted in December 1927 and distraught over the new provincial government that was discarding some of his goals, particularly the establishment of farmers' associations and the adoption of a 25-percent-rent-reduction plan, Shen returned to his village of Yaqian. There in his native East Township he began his own experiment in what generally came to be called rural reconstruction. That meant establishing mass organizations (of farmers, merchants, unskilled laborers, construction workers, and women) and undertaking reconstruction (building irrigation facilities and roads) and reforms (establishing a self-government association, setting up credit and retail cooperatives, building schools, and sponsoring sericulture reforms) within the township. It was an effort to start the reconstruction of China from the grassroots. But Shen did not have enough time: He was assassinated on the afternoon of 28 August 1928.

In interpreting the life of Shen during the revolution of the 1920s, there are several challenges presented by culture and context. The first is an aspect of Chinese political culture. Shen commented on it in an essay in 1919: "I know that ultimately for the Chinese people the name is more important than the deed."[16] Throughout Chinese history many people contended that action or deeds had to be brought to fit the name; there was no sense that names should be changed to fit the action. When Confucius analyzed the disharmony in Chinese society, he found part of the reason to be that people were not doing what their names prescribed. The son must be a son; the father must be a father. If a father tries to be a friend to his son instead of a father, there will be problems. A ruler must be a ruler and not allow others to make decisions for him. In other words, the name prescribed the action that the named should perform. This obviously conservative Confucian idea is referred to as the "rectification of names." In the twentieth century, this obsession with names reached its peak during Mao's Cultural Revolution when society was divided between the red (good) and black (bad) forces. No matter what his actions, if he were the son or grandson of a landlord (black), he would always be ranked with the landlords as an enemy of the people; on the other hand, however bad their actions, the offspring of the proletariat (red) would always be good.

How does this tyranny of names make analyzing Shen more challenging? Every person in every culture has multiple identities stemming from the various roles that he or she plays and the various relationships that he or she maintains. These identities come from oneself (emerging from personality, goals, abilities, lifestyle, particular incidents); from connections to others; and from others who choose for whatever reason to bestow a particular identity upon one. In Chinese culture, more than in the West, those identities that emerge from connections to others are often decisive in helping fix one's identity. Shen was a part of at least seven networks—the extended family, the native-place connections in Yaqian and East Township, the provincial assembly colleagues, the Shanghai intellectuals, the graduates of Hangzhou's First Normal School whom Shen brought to teach at his school, the provincial Guomindang hierarchy, and the Western Hills faction. In addition, Shen had countless connections of greater or lesser strength with others. Shen himself said it in a poem:

> Within the mirror there I am.
> Outside the mirror there I am.
> When I break the mirror, I don't see me.
> The broken fragments of the mirror become pieces of me.
> When I break the mirror, I am nowhere in the mirror.
> When I break the mirror, I have even broken me.
> When I have broken me, I don't know how many of me there are. [17]

In any culture, to be sure, identity is best seen as "process, . . . performance, and . . . provisional." [18] But with the necessity for continual *guanxi* construction, nurturing, repair, and repayment, the fluidity that we have noted as a crucial aspect of Chinese society made the question of identity even more difficult to come to terms with. If we put that fluidity into the context of revolution, which is marked by instability and contingency, fixing identities for a biographical subject becomes extraordinarily challenging. The temptation is to follow the lead of contemporaries trying to deal with that biographical subject: "In the great complexity of revolutionary change, the human mind brings order by naming and holding to that name as the key to the identity of the other. The sense of 'once-named, always-known' becomes the easiest way for individuals to order their world; though it is certainly possible, it then becomes extraordinarily difficult to change the key."[19] Thus, as Shen's identity was continuing to shift amid the twists and turns of revolution, other Chinese, already valuing the noun over the verb, pegged Shen in certain ways—landlord, elite leader, rent-resistance agitator, Western Hills reactionary—many names having sinister overtones, depending on the political viewpoint.

The crucial underlying reality here was the extraordinarily politicized nature of Chinese society that tended to color most naming and most identities. When I went to Yaqian in 1993 to visit Shen's grave, the local officials at first demurred, saying, "We don't yet know whether Shen was a good or bad man." This was sixty-five years after Shen's death. Some of that indecision was a result of Shen's controversial history (son of a landlord, associated with a reactionary political faction but a radical thinker and reformer). But most came from the highly charged politicization of daily life in the People's Republic. In 1966, during the first year of Mao's Cultural Revolution, farmers blasted Shen's mountainside grave open, yanked out his corpse, and threw it down the mountain; at the same time Shen's family was dispossessed and forced to take shelter in a Buddhist compound. Even in my 1993 interview with Shen's son and grandson in the presence of a local Communist cadre, I was warned not to probe too deeply into Shen's life or the affairs of his family. The issue was not knowing what tomorrow's politics might be: One could not step boldly ahead when the ground beneath the current political line might turn to quicksand overnight.

In terms of writing a biography of Shen, the point is this: If Shen's identity and historical significance were still so indeterminable in 1993, how much more uncertain were they among his contemporaries in the 1910s and 1920s? Yet it was those very contemporaries who ascribed to Shen many of his identities and names and have left most of the historical records with which we have to evaluate him. Most of those people wrote from the vantage point of later times when they knew what Shen would never know—the end results of the developments of the 1920s. Surely that knowledge also shaped and colored their depiction of Shen and his times. Given these circumstances, determining Shen Dingyi's most appropriate identity is a mystery not easily solved. Careful (sometimes tentative) judgment of sources, including Shen's own writings and public records, is the key to getting as close to an answer as possible. Important in understanding the "doing" of a biography of a Chinese subject are the difficulties arising from both culture and context.

To bring the issues of culture and context into sharper focus as they shaped Chinese lives and my study of Shen Dingyi, I focus here on his involvement with the Western Hills faction, and his assassination. Of all Shen's actions during his controversial career, none is more puzzling than his participation in the Western Hills meeting in late 1925. Here he was—less than half a decade away from being a founding member of the Communist party, from supporting socialism and feminism, from sponsoring a rent-resistance movement against his fellow landlord elites—now joining with men who were known as the most ideologically reactionary men in the Guomindang. And yet, from his later actions, we know that he had not given up his progressive ideas. As I put it in an essay title, "What's a Man Like You Doing in a Group Like This?"[20] Even the Western Hills group did not believe that he was for real: Three days before the meeting opened, Shen and his close friend Dai Jitao were kidnapped from their hotel and beaten by ultraconservative Guomindang goons who believed that Shen was a Communist agent attending the meeting as a mole.

The Western Hills faction has traditionally been cast primarily in ideological terms. Though most who attended this meeting were conservative, there was a range of ideological viewpoints. Ideological commitment was not the basis or raison d'être for the meeting. It was instead concerned with practical revolutionary politics. The proceedings of the conference show that the men came together because of specific political grievances at a particular historical moment. These grievances included the power of the chief Soviet adviser, Borodin, in party affairs; the continuing membership of Communists in the Guomindang; and the collaboration of the leader of the Guomindang Left, Wang Jingwei, with the Communists.

Apart from the existential political situation, what brought this particular group together? Here, connections and networks take center stage. An analysis of Western Hills participants' various connections (native-place ties, kinship and marital ties, friendships, political patron-client ties, shared voluntary association memberships, and shared revolutionary experiences) reveals that there were two networks. Shen's network was composed of four men who were linked by common native place, professional background, and friendship. They were clearly more moderate than the majority of the Western Hills group. On the political grievances aired at the meeting, this network was more tolerant of Borodin's leadership, was not ready to support a unilateral break with the Communists, and did not favor a backlash against Wang Jingwei. All four in this network left the meeting early. With reference to the main network, they were clearly peripheral both organizationally and in strength of post-conference commitment. This main network of eleven men was made up of two clusters, one linked by friendship and common work in political associations, the other by friendship, native-place ties, and being disciples of an early twentieth-century revolutionary leader. These eleven signed a letter to Wang Jingwei detailing why the Communists had to be ousted from the Guomindang. Thus analysis of connections and networks seem, at least in this case, to provide more appropriate explanations for conference attendance than assuming that these men were all like-minded reactionaries.

Shen, as best we can tell, attended the meeting in large part because of the personal connection of friendship; if Dai had not attended the meeting, it is not likely that Shen would have gone. In addition, he attended in part because of a genuine concern about growing Soviet and Communist power in the Chinese revolution. Finally there was likely a personal career motive: His distrust of Communists derived in part from his being challenged for leadership in the Zhejiang provincial Guomindang by idealistic, driven young men, fifteen to twenty years his junior, who had once been his disciples and were also Communist party members. These young men saw Shen's attendance at the conference as the first volley in a bitter political war that would last into the spring of 1927 when, following the Northern Expedition, Chiang Kai-shek would kill or imprison Shen's challengers in the general White Terror that he unleashed.

In the end, Shen came out over his rivals, not through his actions but through the course of revolution. In the summer and fall of 1927 he headed the anti-Communist purge in Zhejiang and was a key figure in the provincial government in the fall. Throughout this period, however, he labored under the new identity that his attendance at the Western Hills conference had given him among his contemporaries—that of ultraconservative. It did not matter that that name had no connection to the reality of Shen's actions or thought. It did not seem to matter when he undertook the radically reformist rural reconstruction program in 1928. For his enemies, the name became a political weapon; for those who had always thought Shen was unpredictable, the name was corroborative. For his friends, it was mystifying. For these reasons, Shen's involvement with the Western Hills group from November 1925 to April 1926 had "drastic and permanent implications for his image and his future. . . . It was a stigma that Shen could not in the end overcome."[21] How strong the connection of Shen was with the Western Hills group is shown by the popular name of the Hangzhou house of Shen's relative in which Shen met with fellow Guomindang members in late 1927: the "Western Hills Zhejiang Garrison."

On 28 August 1928, after more than six months working at his rural reconstruction experiment, Shen was assassinated in Yaqian on returning from Moganshan, a resort north of Hangzhou. On the spur of the moment, he had gone to meet several leaders of the Guomindang, one of them being Dai Jitao, whom he had not seen since their joint Western Hills conference attendance almost three years earlier. He did not know how long he would stay in Moganshan or when he would return. Three days later, on his return trip, after he took a ferry across the Qiantang River from Hangzhou, he boarded a bus for the forty-five-minute ride from the river depot to Yaqian, and his killers boarded the bus with him. They killed him after he got off the bus in Yaqian.

As Shen's assassination had never been solved, I set out to solve it, writing the biography as a murder mystery. Indeed, attempting to solve the case uses the skills of a detective, but the solution comes straight out of Chinese cultural dynamics at this moment in history—connections and networks, questions of social identity and social fluidity—and also from the joker in any historical deck, contingency. The case does not lack suspects. Shen had made many enemies during his career: local landlords, provincial assembly opponents, Communist party members, Guomindang leftists. Even on the private, personal level Shen's arrogance and brashness had created enemies. In an account of his death, the Shanghai newspaper *Shenbao* asserted that "Shen's natural disposition was that he made arbitrary decisions on his own and that he was continually in disagreement with people."[22]

There were five major suspects, two of whom could be dispensed with rather quickly. One was a Buddhist monk, outraged at Shen because his temple had been seized during the rent-resistance movement in 1921 and had been made the headquarters for the Alliance of Farmers' Associations. Over the years he had repeatedly made threats and reportedly accumulated "hit" money to do Shen in. But the key to the killers' identities was that the actual perpetrators of the murder had boarded the same bus as Shen: That development underscores the fact that whoever masterminded the assassination knew of Shen's travel plans and schedule and had at their disposal some substantial organizational abilities. The Buddhist monk would have had no way of knowing about Shen's return, since, as I have said, Shen had not planned it. The same can be said of silkworm merchants, often mentioned as suspects because their livelihood was threatened by the sericulture reform sponsored by Shen in his rural reconstruction effort. They may have had a motive but not the means or resources to pull the killing off. Stronger suspects were local landlords, who remained bitter about Shen's masterminding of the rent-resistance movement in 1921 and about his strident support for the 25-percent-rent-reduction effort. They were very suspicious about his rural reconstruction effort, which was rumored to include some scheme for land redistribution. They had the wherewithal to arrange the killing, but the timing is problematic: Unless they had links to someone at Moganshan who was aware of Shen's decision to leave and who knew what time he had left, they would not have been able to coordinate the plan. Since one man arrested in the case confessed that a landlord had hired him to kill Shen, the possibility exists that a landlord had served as middleman and hired the killer. However, we will never know because the confessor ended up mysteriously murdered in his prison cell.

Communists obviously had motives to do away with Shen. His leadership of the anti-Communist purge the year before gave them a strong grievance. But their involvement was not logical. At this point they were demoralized, bankrupt, and, for all practical purposes, defunct. Why would they have expended precious resources on a man who no longer had any provincial power and had antagonized so many people that he would likely never be brought back into the power elite? The timing is also a problem. Why would they have used this plan, the timing of which was tricky at best, when they could have chosen any number of public meetings at which Shen appeared?

Men in Shen's own party, Chiang Kai-shek's Guomindang, had the motives and the wherewithal to carry out Shen's murder. We are led to them by those elements of Chinese culture that have been the focus of this paper: networks, the power of names, and the fluidity of identity in the revolutionary context. Two questions need to be addressed: Who was behind the assassination; and why now, when Shen's political power was weaker than it had been earlier in the decade? The answer to the first question is based on circumstantial but compelling evidence. The "who" question goes back to the bus ride of Shen and his killers: How did the killers know Shen would be on that bus? Since Shen himself did not know until the morning of 28 August that he was returning to Yaqian, one of the four Guomindang officials staying at the Moganshan resort had to have sent messages to set the assassination plot in motion. No one else would have known Shen's departure time. There are other circumstantial clues. In the weeks prior to the assassination, Shen had received two warnings about his rural reconstruction self-government project from a former Zhejiang official and from the current head of the provincial Guomindang, Zhang Jingjiang, a close confidant of Chiang Kai-shek. Chiang, who also hailed from Zhejiang Province, had disliked Shen from the beginning of their acquaintance, had never accepted him in any of his networks, and had treated him indifferently and kept him at arm's length. The party's warnings cautioned Shen to curb his radicalism and outspokenness.

Further, the post-assassination coldness of the Guomindang suggests that the party was glad to be rid of Shen. Chiang refused requests for a state funeral and for the appointment of a special court to hear the case. The provincial government said that the East Township rural reconstruction project could remain as a permanent memorial to Shen; but it shut it down in little more than a year. At a large exposition in Hangzhou in 1929, party leaders rejected out of hand the request that Shen should be included as a martyr in the Memorial Hall of the Revolution.

The question of "why now" brings us to issues of Chinese culture. We know there was concern in the party about Shen's "radical" self-government experiment. At a time when Chiang Kai-shek's White Terror was unabated and when the party's revolutionary goals had not yet been accomplished, Shen's alternative strategy of rural reconstruction likely seemed threatening in its dissent. Many people wondered whether Shen was simply trying to build a base for himself from which he might plan military action. Rumors about Shen's plans spread rapidly. A photograph of a rack for fire-fighting equipment was taken to be a gun rack for a rumored township militia said to be twenty-thousand-strong. Quarriers on Phoenix Mountain at Yaqian were said to be building a military garrison. In a premodern culture, such as China's was at this time and earlier, rumor was "the news" and almost always played a major role in determining what people thought about their world.

Part of Shen's difficulty was that he had allowed connections to party leaders and participation in national and even provincial networks to lapse; this stemmed from his focus from 1925 to 1927 on his battle with the leftists for control of the province, a struggle waged mostly in local county bureaus. Thus, he had no strong *guanxi* to ensure his own safety and standing. Dai Jitao was one of those lapsed connections, and a tragic lapse it was. Then Shen compounded his difficulties by making the mistake of being boldly frank with Dai at Moganshan. He had reportedly told his erstwhile friend, "The revolution that originally rose in people's hearts has not been satisfied. Because the situation was [originally] unsatisfactory, we had to have a revolution. But the present unsatisfied nature of people's hearts means that there must be another revolution."[23] Such blunt talk must have signaled imminent danger to Dai, at that time a key member of the Guomindang's leadership group; sources tell us that Dai abruptly cut the conversation short. Thus it is possible that part of the motive for the murder was to eliminate this radical before he could make serious trouble.

But the "why now" question seems to rise out of culture and context; the reason was likely Shen's very trip to Moganshan. Of the four party officials at the resort, one was a Western Hills faction leader named Zhang who had been in the core network at the Western Hills meeting, and another was a military man named Li from a faction called the Guangxi clique. In the fall of 1927 the Western Hills faction had been aligned with the Guangxi clique. Both faction and clique were opponents of Chiang Kai-shek. In the summer of 1928 rumors had begun to spread that anti-Chiang ferment was brewing among members of the Guangxi clique. The coincidence of Li's and Zhang's visits at such a time may have raised some suspicion, but to have Shen—also of the Western Hills group—come to Moganshan (even though ostensibly to see Dai) was troubling. Two Chinese analyses (both from the "historical materials" sources and studded with factual errors) suggest that Shen's trip to Moganshan at that particular moment was the critical act leading to his assassination because "it stirred up the Western Hills-related suspicions of Chiang Kai-shek, who would likely have been notified of Shen's visit by Dai Jitao."[24] Dai may have interpreted Shen's call for another revolution as one that would be led by a Guangxi and Western Hills alliance.

An account by a Communist labor organizer at the time alleges that the killer was hired on Chiang Kai-shek's orders to one of his main generals. This is also the story that Shen's family gave me in interviews in 1993. If true, "the sad and ironic fact is that Shen seems to have been killed because he was perceived as too radical and as too reactionary at the same time by the same party."[25] The continuing perception of Shen as a Western Hills partisan was in all likelihood the proximate cause of his murder: Once a member of the Western Hills networks, always a member of the Western Hills networks. The family did not understand why Shen attended the Western Hills meeting, but the cultural hegemony of name persisted. About this judgment by the party, Shen's son wrote, "They put the hat of the extreme rightist counterrevolutionary Guomindang on his head, and there was no scientific analysis of the specific situation."[26]

I have argued in this chapter that culture and context are crucial perspectives that must be taken into account by the biographer; put briefly, they inform and alert the researcher to elements that might be substantially different or unrecognizable or missing in a different culture and/or in a different context. Not to consider the cultural perspective is to commit the "culture-bound" error of considering one's own culture and worldview as the norm. Not to consider the contextual perspective prevents us from fully understanding the changes over time in our subject's life — some large, but most incremental — and, above all, the importance of contingency in the course of a life.

Yet it is important to stress that culture and context are not everything: They do not necessarily determine the decisions and actions of a person. The biographer must study his subject as an individual person within a particular culture and context, who in the end, under particular circumstances or in certain situations, may or may not play a role in helping shape or confine or direct his actions. In many ways, Shen Dingyi seems culturally quite "atypical" of Chinese — a brash knight-errant, willing (sometimes, it seems, almost eager) to make enemies, relishing the flaunting of tradition, almost reveling in his individuality. Yet, however atypical he seemed, what I continue to find striking about Shen's life and death — his individuality — is how they were shaped by and within the confines of his culture and the contexts in which he acted. We must understand culture and context to know what questions we should ask about him and to interpret appropriately the meaning of his actions and the trajectory of his life.

Notes

1. Robert Rosenstone, "History in Images/History in Words: Reflections on the Possibility of Really Putting History onto Film," *American Historical Review* 93 (December 1988): 1185.

2. John K. Fairbank, "Assignment for the '70s," *American Historical Review* 64 (February 1969): 867.

3. Nell Irvin Painter, *Sojourner Truth, A Life, A Symbol* (New York: W. W. Norton, 1996), 366–68.

4. Miles F. Shore, "Biography in the 1980s: A Psychoanalytic Perspective," *Journal of Interdisciplinary History* 12 (summer 1981): 102.

5. Thomas A. Kohut, "Psychohistory as History," *American Historical Review* 91 (April 1986): 352.

6. Robert Darnton, "Looking the Devil in the Face," *New York Review of Books*, 10 February 2000.

7. "Biographies — New Literary Trend in China," *Beijing Review* 38 (13–19 November 1995): 35.

8. Painter, *Sojourner Truth*, 113.

9. Fox Butterfield, *China: Alive in a Bitter Sea* (New York: Times Books, 1982), 74–75, cited in Ambrose Yeo-chi King, "Kuan-hsi and Network Building," *Daedalus* 120 (spring 1991): 64.

10. Fei Xiaotong, *From the Soil: The Foundations of Chinese Society* (Berkeley and Los Angeles: University of California Press, 1992), 78–79.

11. See Philippe Aries, *Centuries of Childhood: A Social History of Family Life* (New York: Vintage Books, 1962); on adolescence, see Joseph F. Kett, "Adolescence and Youth in Nineteenth-Century America," *Journal of Interdisciplinary History* 2 (autumn 1971): 283–98.

12. Kenneth Keniston, "Psychological Development and Historical Change," *Journal of Interdisciplinary History* 2 (autumn 1971): 342–43.

13. Quotes from Tu Wei-ming, "The Confucian Perception of Adulthood," *Daedalus* 105 (spring 1976): 113, 115.

14. Quoted in Theodore DeBary et al., eds., *Sources of Chinese Tradition* (New York: Columbia University Press, 1960), 1:24.

15. Wang Gungwu, *The Chineseness of China* (Hong Kong and New York: Oxford University Press, 1991), 196.

16. "Mingyi zhong? Shishi zhong?" *Xingqi pinglun* ["Is the name or the deed more important?" *Weekly Review*], 24 August 1919.

17. "Du Dabaide 'Duijing,'" *Juewu* ["On Reading Liu Dabai's 'Facing the Mirror,'" *Awakenings*], 20 September 1920.

18. Liz Bondi, "Locating Identity Politics," in *Place and the Politics of Identity*, ed. Michael Keith and Steve Pile (London: Routledge, 1993), 97.

19. R. Keith Schoppa, *Blood Road. The Mystery of Shen Dingyi in Revolutionary China* (Berkeley and Los Angeles: University of California Press, 1995), 253.

20. R. Keith Schoppa, "Shen Dingyi and the Western Hills Group: 'What's a Man Like You Doing in a Group Like This?' " *Republican China* 16 (November 1990): 35–50.

21. Schoppa, *Blood Road*, 166, 209.

22. *Shenbao*, 3 September 1928.

23. "Shen Dingyi beici jingguo" ["The Assassination of Mr. Shen Dingyi"], (n.d.), unpaginated, Zhehiang Provincial Library, Hangzhou.

24. Schoppa, *Blood Road*, 247.

25. Schoppa, *Blood Road*, 250.

26. Shen Jianyun, letter to author, 30 June 1993.

Selected Bibliography

"Biographies — New Literary Trend in China." *Beijing Review* 38 (13–19 November 1995): 35.

Bondi, Liz. "Locating Identity Politics." In *Place and the Politics of Identity*, ed. Michael Keith and Steve Pile. London: Routledge, 1993.

Darnton, Robert. "Looking the Devil in the Face." *New York Review of Books* (10 February 2000): 14–16.

Fei, Xiaotong. *From the Soil: The Foundations of Chinese Society*. Berkeley and Los Angeles: University of California Press, 1992.

Keniston, Kenneth. "Psychological Development and Historical Change." *Journal of Interdisciplinary History* 2 (autumn 1971): 329–45.

Kett, Joseph F. "Adolescence and Youth in Nineteenth-Century America." *Journal of Interdisciplinary History* 2 (autumn 1971): 283–98.

Kohut, Thomas A. "Psychohistory as History." *American Historical Review* 91 (April 1986): 336–54.

Painter, Nell Irvin. *Sojourner Truth, A Life, A Symbol*. New York: W. W. Norton, 1996.

Rosenstone, Robert. "History in Images/History in Words: Reflections on the Possibility of Really Putting History onto Film." *American Historical Review* 93 (December 1988): 1173–85.

Schoppa, R. Keith. *Blood Road. The Mystery of Shen Dingyi in Revolutionary China*. Berkeley and Los Angeles: University of California Press, 1995.

———. "Shen Dingyi and the Western Hills Group: 'What's a Man Like You Doing in a Group Like This?' " *Republican China* 16 (November 1990): 35–50.

Shore, Miles F. "Biography in the 1980s: A Psychoanalytic Perspective." *Journal of Interdisciplinary History* 12 (summer 1981): 89–113.

Tu, Wei-ming. "The Confucian Perception of Adulthood." *Daedalus* 105 (spring 1976): 109–24.

3. Reshaping Tudor Biography: Anne Boleyn and Anne of Cleves

Retha M. Warnicke

Recapturing the history of Englishwomen is difficult, for the great majority of them can only be glimpsed briefly in court records; other official documents, such as wills; parish registers; or the letters of their male relatives. It is only from the late sixteenth century that some women's diaries and journals have survived. Despite this limited and inadequate evidence, a great interest emerged among professional historians in the 1970s in researching the lives of medieval as well as modern Englishwomen. It took another decade before historians turned seriously to studying the lives of early modern Englishwomen, essentially those who lived from the sixteenth to the eighteenth centuries. In their 1998 study of early modern Englishwomen, Sara Mendelson and Patricia Crawford referred to the neglect of this period as the "Dark Ages of women's history."[1]

The findings of Mendelson and Crawford have contributed significantly to the history of elite women and even to that of poor women, although there is far less direct evidence for the latter, most of whom were illiterate. All women, regardless of their social rank in this hierarchical society, shared common life experiences, partly because the fundamental structure of society—politically, socially, economically, and culturally—was based on a clear division between the sexes. Women were considered the inferior sex, were deemed more lecherous than men, and were expected to accept subordination to a patriarchal authority: a father, a husband, a brother, or another male guardian. Even the rule of Queen Elizabeth I, as A. N. McLaren has recently pointed out, was accepted and justified by her councillors and many members of Parliament only insofar as she could be seen to be receptive to the counsel of her male advisers.[2]

Because the field of early modern women's history is relatively new, the need to review and restructure previous studies that make reference to women is great. Sometimes the women's voices are all but muted; at other times the text is either biased or filled with an inaccurate understanding of their shared social experiences. More specifically, the reshaping of the biographies of Tudor women, which, because of the extant evidence, necessarily involves only the elite women of the sixteenth century, falls within this larger historical context. Even for them, archival collections are generally disappointing because they not only contain relatively few personal manuscripts but they also house a variety of public documents that are riddled with fabrications. In contrast to the scarcity and unreliability of these contemporary records, the number of secondary sources is overwhelming, since for more than four hundred years authors have been publishing books about the people of this pivotal century that encompassed both the English Renaissance and the Reformation. After exploring the problems in interpreting these original and secondary sources, this essay will address the often-repeated truism that composing Tudor biographies is problematic because not enough personal evidence has survived to create a portrait of the subject's character. Ultimately, of course, the processing of this data requires the adoption of the careful research methods that are commonly used for larger historical surveys.

Many of the existing life stories of Tudor women serve mainly to authenticate manifold layers of negative gender bias. This bias, given the actuality of Tudor gender relationships, is understandably present in the archives, but it is also rife in early modern secondary sources and even in more recent histories. This modern threefold bias exists partly because of the way in which historical studies developed in the late nineteenth century. As the field of English history became professionalized, it retreated from the amateur's part-time venture to a male-dominated, scientifically oriented academic exercise that almost exclusively valued archival evidence for recovering the past within legal, diplomatic, and economic narratives. Under the "illusion" that "facts speak for themselves,"[3] these Victorians purposely limited their analyses of the documents' origins and contents, sometimes quoting "lengthy" and "undigested"[4] excerpts from them.[5] In tune with their culture's marginalization of women, they not only rarely allowed for a gender bias in the archives and in the early modern secondary sources but also underestimated the importance of women's lives,[6] often ignoring their contributions entirely.

Except in the cases of some major political figures, such as Henry VIII or Elizabeth I, these historians, as well as their early twentieth-century successors, mostly eschewed biographies. They based their careers and built their scholarly reputations upon grander surveys.[7] Valuing the "great scene," they denigrated as a "trivial" exercise the "study of a single individual and the slight thread of happenings" that formed her or his life. They regarded biography as being at most a minor subfield within historical studies; some even characterized it as a "province of literature."[8] Sir John Neale, for example, who earned a knighthood for his only biography, the 1934 study of Queen Elizabeth I, is best known in academia for his numerous parliamentary investigations.[9]

At least one modern historian has even denied that a biography of a key Tudor figure should or even could be composed. Throughout his career, G. R. Elton, the dean of early Tudor studies, declined to write a full biography of Thomas Cromwell, the principal secretary and Lord Privy Seal of Henry VIII who was executed in 1540, because so little information has survived about his childhood and adolescence.[10] These gaps in Cromwell's life led Elton to believe that an analysis of Cromwell's career from a close reading of the public documents was as much as we could understand of the man whom he identified as the architect of the English Reformation.

As late-twentieth-century Tudor historians have increasingly turned to writing biographies, which, for the reading public, is the most popular nonfiction genre,[11] they have often failed to take advantage of the advances made in women's history, the history of sexuality, or family history. For example, in 1986, when the established scholar E. W. Ives decided to publish a biography of Anne Boleyn, he chose to frame her life using a version of C. S. Lewis's outdated theory of courtly love that was derived from medieval romances. Almost no other scholar today argues, as Ives has done, that it was an actual, accepted practice at court for older, married women, like Anne Boleyn, to have intimate, potentially sexual relationships with younger men. A reading of women's history and of up-to-date literary criticism would have alerted him to the inaccuracies of this conceptualization. [12]

In his positive reassessment in 1959 of the naval career of the duke of Medina Sidonia, commander of the unsuccessful Armada in 1588, Garrett Mattingly said: "Nor does it matter at all to the dead whether they receive justice at the hands of the succeeding generations. But to the living, to do justice, however belatedly, should matter." [13] Mattingly's belief that it should "matter" to "do justice" to the "dead" stands as an inspiration for expunging the long-term and deeply ingrained biases from women's life stories. This reshaping will result in replacing stereotypical images of Tudor women as manipulators of men's passions or as mere victims of their society with more rational and complex biographical portraits. Until this task is accomplished, women's cultural contributions will remain hidden; as Robin Winks has said, "Someone ought to be interested in finding out the truth about things, for the truth ought to matter." [14] Surely, searching for the "truth" about half of the population "ought to matter."

Another reason for this reshaping is that, as long as the gender bias dominates women's life stories, an analysis of men's actions must remain incomplete and inadequate. For example, if the events of Anne Boleyn's life continue to hinge on this centuries-old bias, a valid interpretation of her career at court and her relationship to Henry VIII will be impossible. The present scholarly opinion offers two scenarios for the execution of Anne, his apparently flirtatious second wife, and her accused lovers. Either he sought to facilitate his courting of Jane Seymour, soon to become his third consort, knowing full well that Anne and the men were innocent of the charges, or he actually believed that the alleged adulterous behavior, viewed through the lenses of witchcraft, was the reason for Anne's January miscarriage and perhaps the deformity of her aborted fetus.

A definitive answer to the mystery of her death, as John Foxe character-ized it, [15] cannot be found in the archives; the royal family, as J. H. Plumb has remarked, inhabited an "enclosed, narrow world" and maintained "zones of silence" about personal matters.[16] That the court's secrets re-mained impenetrable to outside observation is unfortunate because the difference in the analysis of Henry's and Anne's characters that these two theories evoke are enormous and far-reaching. On the one hand, either Anne was a flirtatious woman who refused to take her position as the crowned queen of England seriously, or she failed in her primary task of presenting the king with a healthy male heir. On the other hand, either he knowingly had six innocent people executed to sate his lust for Jane Seymour, or he acted out of ignorance of the natural laws of human reproduction. The more probable explanation, given the cultural attitudes of early modern Christendom, is that he assented to Anne's death be-cause he believed her immoral activities had led to the miscarriage of her fetus.[17]

Another reason for reshaping Tudor biography is that until recently historians of Protestantism, who interpreted the reformed movement as a progressive event in accordance with the Whig view of history, dominated historical writing. John Foxe's providential tales of the Protestant martyrs of Queen Mary's reign have influenced analyses of the Reformation to the current period.[18] A. G. Dickens's study of English Protestantism in 1964, for example, offered his readers the deterministic view that it was an inevitable and intrinsically superior religious movement. In his deeply felt argument, Dickens remarked: "Even if Henry VIII had remained a model of matrimonial respectability, even if the ministers of Edward VI had been converted by a stray Jesuit, even if Queen Mary had survived for another decade, it still requires a vivid imagination to envisage the English as dutiful children of the Holy See at the end of the century."[19] Using oceanic imagery, he characterized English Catholicism as "an old unseaworthy and ill-commanded galleon."[20]

This historical view of Protestantism as an inevitable or providential movement has shaped the depictions of the Tudors. Both Anne Boleyn and Anne of Cleves, Henry VIII's second and fourth wives, for example, loom inaccurately in some accounts as facilitators of Protestant doctrine.[21] This approach has also marred studies of Henry VIII's daughters, Mary and Elizabeth. The Victorian scholar James A. Froude viewed Elizabeth as a great stumbling block to the advancement of reform: "With malicious enjoyment," he reported, she frustrated "good honest men" who differed with her. Although historians have recently been revising or refuting this deterministic view, it still pervades many studies of the period, and Queen Mary is best known by the negative Protestant epithet of "bloody."[22]

A final reason for reshaping Tudor biographies, particularly that of Anne of Cleves, is the failure of earlier historians to use German sources that discuss events at the Henrician court. Other evidence, mostly English and French, seems to identify Cromwell as an ally of the Cleves dukedom. A study of the dispatches of its ad hoc ambassador to England in 1540, however, reveals a strained relationship between Cromwell and the agents of Cleves.[23] The German understanding of court politics has failed to receive the attention it merits because the fragmented country was still divided into many principalities, none of which exchanged resident ambassadors with England, as did France and Spain. In addition, the German archives concerning English diplomacy, unlike those of France and Spain, are less extensive and remain largely untranslated.

In the remainder of this essay, I shall first examine three specific kinds of evidence that need to be reevaluated in reshaping Tudor biographies: fiction in the archives,[24] deliberate distortions in early modern secondary accounts, and the misrepresentation of rituals in modern histories. Then I shall explain some of my biographical methods, with specific references to Anne Boleyn and Anne of Cleves, including how I chose my subjects and how I conceptualized and structured their life stories.

Inevitably, Tudor historians must rely upon inadequate archives for their research projects. Compared with those of most other European countries, England's archives are plentiful and indexed, but unfortunately, they contain few documents with personal data beyond some information about the individuals' public careers, their activities in courts of law, and their interaction with other governmental agencies. While it is true that vital statistics are normally available for reigning monarchs, that data is often not readily accessible for other members of the royal family or members of the aristocracy. The major reason for this lack of information is that it was not until 1538 that parishes began to maintain registers of births, deaths, and marriages. Until recently, for example, the birth year of Henry VIII's sister, Mary, who was born in 1496 and wed Louis XII of France in 1514, remained a mystery. Finally, it was found entered, almost as an afterthought, in a Book of Hours.[25] Historians speculate that the birth year of Anne Boleyn ranges from 1500 to 1507. The age attributed to Henry VIII's fifth queen, Catherine Howard, relies in part on the supposition that in 1540, when the king was forty-nine, he surely would not have wed a woman younger than eighteen. This argument has gained credibility despite the fact that in late 1537 and during most of 1538, he seriously considered marrying Emperor Charles V's young niece, Christina, duchess of Milan, who was born in February 1522.[26]

Some of the archival records are actually misleading about the personal lives of the royal family. Too many of the references to them in resident ambassadors' correspondence, for example, have gained an unmerited credibility in historical accounts. By the early sixteenth century, England regularly exchanged resident ambassadors with Paris and Madrid; their task was to report back to their principals all the information they could gather, much of it from bribed sources. Usually ignorant of the English language, foreign ambassadors in London had to communicate with both the Tudor family and Crown officials in French and Latin. The diplomats' ability to validate the facts they gathered was thus greatly limited, and they seemed not to have been overly concerned about corroborating the many conjectures and rumors that they faithfully recorded.[27] That their news mostly represented what royal officials wanted them to know should always be considered when relying upon them for evidence. It is somewhat problematic, for example, to believe, as some do, that Thomas Cromwell was actually leaking valid confidential information to Eustace Chapuys, the Spanish/Imperial resident ambassador when, as England's principal secretary, Cromwell was supporting Henry's decision to obtain an annulment of his marriage to Catherine of Aragon, an aunt of Emperor Charles V. The information in Chapuys's correspondence, sometimes even within the same dispatch, is contradictory and almost always derogatory when referring to members of the royal family, except Catherine and her daughter Mary. Naturally, the news that Chapuys wanted to learn, and did learn from his bribed sources, was that Anne Boleyn was a she-wolf and an Agrippina. If this bewitching woman could be expelled from court, Chapuys speculated wistfully, then certainly Henry would return to Catherine.

Later, after the king had wed Anne, the hostile ambassador referred to her as the royal concubine.[28]

Because Chapuys's dispatches are so full of news, which, however, is mostly misinformation, historians have relied on them extensively. His records formed the major primary source for Paul Friedmann's full-length, two-volume biography of Anne Boleyn in 1884. Friedmann, who claimed that the diplomats "spoke the truth or what they believed to be the truth," accepted whole cloth every scurrilous story about Anne that Chapuys reported to his correspondents. These biased documents, which Friedmann considered "of the greatest value," still shape how some modern historians approach her life.[29]

Other important, but equally biased, evidence can be found in judicial records. In his important studies of criminal trials in early modern England, Malcolm Gaskill has pointed out that deponents who believed that a particular event had occurred chose to explain their beliefs through fabricated or invented narratives, which the justices accepted as valid even when the testimony contained supernatural allegations. Gaskill characterized this as sincere behavior that arose from a different "ordering of reality in the early modern period . . . a lost social context of communication" that slowly disappeared after 1700.[30] His findings are reminders of how important it is for researchers to determine which data in the judicial records are false; the evidence requires careful analysis to discover, whenever possible, where facts end and fiction begins. Two famous cases in which fabricated evidence is an important issue involve the failed royal marriages of Anne Boleyn and Anne of Cleves. In 1536 the Crown charged Anne Boleyn with enticing five men, each on two separate occasions, to have sexual relations with her at specific places between October 1533 and December 1535. The ten dates are problematic for, even with the paucity of extant evidence, it can be proved with certainty that at some of those times she was not at the places specified. For example, her brother, George, Lord Rochford, stood accused of having committed incest with her at Westminster on 5 November 1535, but irrefutable evidence places her with Henry at Windsor on that day.[31]

The king's annulment from Anne of Cleves in July 1540 greatly relied on depositions with fictional information. Especially significant to Anne of

Cleves's life story is the one signed by three of her ladies-in-waiting. The critical evidence Crown attorneys needed to support the king's case was Anne's confirmation of his failure to consummate their marriage. Asking Anne, who still mainly spoke German, about her evenings with the king to get legal evidence to end the union that she hoped to preserve would have proved awkward at best. Instead, three of Anne's ladies signed a deposition detailing some conversations with her that supposedly took place but without an interpreter present. Her allegedly innocent responses to their questions about whether or not she was pregnant provided evidence of her complete misunderstanding of how conception occurs. Writers who have validated the details of this deposition have not only ignored the problem of language barriers that would have prevented these conversations from occurring—at least as they were reported—but also other references that indicate that Anne was quite well aware of what a woman's "bodily integrity" was. In fact, in January 1540, shortly after her marriage to Henry, she had attempted on several occasions to converse privately with Cromwell about her marital problems, but he had refused her requests. Since knowledge of Henry's incapacity is largely based on letters Cromwell later addressed to him, it would certainly have been interesting to the details of Anne of Cleves's life if Cromwell had discussed with her those trying times with the king.[32]

Forged documents, especially letters, offer another kind of archival fiction. Three letters that Anne Boleyn allegedly wrote, for example, are almost certainly forgeries. It is entirely likely that the seventeenth-century Catholic writer Gregorio Leti either created or mistranslated two of them to prove her guilty, in the Chapuys tradition, of lasciviously destroying Henry's union with Catherine of Aragon. These two documents reveal her as aggressively seeking to wed Henry and as contemplating avenging the perceived wrongs of his minister, Thomas, Cardinal Wolsey, who did not favor her marriage. Most scholars now recognize them as forgeries primarily because Leti's transcripts are the earliest version of them.[33]

A third alleged letter of Anne's can be traced somewhat further back in time but only to an Elizabethan transcript. She supposedly sent this message to Henry after he had ordered her imprisoned in the Tower of London for adultery with five men. The document has inaccurate information and alludes to his "fancy" for other women, a charge that she was unlikely to make in a message pleading for justice and clemency. Furthermore, at the Tower the king's officials monitored her activities closely and prevented her from sending communications abroad. [34]

Like the Leti documents, this Elizabethan letter is probably a forgery, but it is possible that the intent of its author was not so malicious as Leti's seems to have been. The Elizabethan transcript could have been a product of educational practice in the premodern world. It was the custom, as can be seen from Lady Grace Mildmay's youthful experience, for tutors to require their pupils to compose letters to improve their writing skills. It was also one of three usual domestic activities, the other two being needlework and Scripture reading, that their guardians assigned to girls to prevent them from falling into the idleness that bred wicked thoughts and deeds. [35] Some students could have composed letters that they believed famous people, such as Anne Boleyn, might have written. B. A. Lees has determined, for example, that the letters allegedly written by Eleanor of Aquitaine to Pope Celestine III were instead created in a schoolroom. [36]

Besides fictitious archival statements, misinformation in numerous secondary early modern accounts has entered the infrastructure of Tudor biographies. Thomas More's portrait of Richard III with a misshapen back and Nicholas Sander's depiction of Anne Boleyn with six fingers and a wen have come to frame their lives. Except in the case of Richard III, these accounts have usually implanted a more negative attitude toward female than male subjects. Sander, a Catholic priest who wrote several decades after Anne's death, almost certainly reversed the neo-Platonic ideal in drawing up his now famous description of her, since no extant contemporary record describes her with irregular features. To disparage her and her daughter, Elizabeth, the Protestant queen of England, he created Anne's fictitious body, which outwardly represented the evil that he believed permeated the core of her inner self. In this example, his gender bias reinforced and intersected with a religious bias that resulted in the creation of a monstrous, witchlike woman. [37]

Another example of a religious bias informing a gender bias can be found in the work of Gilbert Burnet, bishop of Salisbury, the late seventeenth-century Protestant historian of the English Reformation.

Burnet had valid reasons for favoring the marriage of Henry and Anne of Cleves in 1540 since her brother-in-law, Frederick, duke elector of Saxony, was a principal leader of the German Lutherans. The king's successful union with Anne could have greatly solidified English contacts with German reformers and, from Burnet's point of view, could have led to the Protestant conversion of England at an earlier date than that at which it actually occurred. In his disappointment at the marriage's failure, the bishop chose to ridicule and demean Anne's looks. Having noted that, upon viewing her for the first time, Henry questioned whether she was as "fair" as others had claimed, Burnet labeled her a "Flander's Mare" and charged the great artist, Hans Holbein the Younger, with having painted a flattering portrait of her to deceive the king. No contemporary evidence supports these assertions. Several eyewitnesses referred to her as beautiful, and Nicholas Wotton, an English ambassador who in 1539 viewed both Holbein's portrait and Anne's visage, judged that it was a realistic image of her. Just as important to the refutation of the bishop's accusations, which were not written until well more than one hundred years after the marriage ended, is the career of Holbein, whom Henry continued to employ as an artist until Holbein died from natural causes.[38]

Modern biographers of Tudor women have, with few exceptions, indiscriminately blended gender bias in the archives with gender bias in the secondary sources. Most writers quote Burnet's statements about Anne of Cleves verbatim, as though he were one of her contemporaries. On the other hand, since Sander's description of Anne Boleyn's body was truly excessive, scholars have often reduced her sixth finger to an extra fingernail and her wen to a mole.[39] In these works, the woman's looks, motivations, goals, and significance lie buried under centuries of fictions. Freeing Anne Boleyn and Anne of Cleves, among others, from this bias in which they are judged largely by their appearance is a serious and ongoing enterprise, and much work has yet to be done.

In addition to authenticating the fiction in the archives and validating the erroneous claims of early modern accounts, some biographers, in processing evidence from Tudor rites of passage, have committed the error that Robin Winks warned against when he said, "It is profoundly unhistorical to read back our habits and behavior into an age many hundred years past."[40] Part of the confusion arises from the assumption that Christian practices have remained constant over time, but just the opposite is true. For example, today's parents, as well as godparents, when it is relevant, attend the christenings of infants, and widowed spouses routinely participate in public funeral services. Early modern protocol was different, especially with reference to the royal family.

First, as to christenings, since new mothers remained secluded in their lying-in chambers until up to forty days after childbirth, they were unable to attend the first rites of their infants, who were usually christened when they were a few days old. Moreover, since the children, especially in royal christenings, held the premier place in the ritual, monarchs, who would necessarily upstage them by their presence, had to be absent. Thus, although historians have claimed that Henry was disappointed with Elizabeth's sex, his dismay was not the reason he did not attend her christening; custom required his absence. To prove this assertion it is necessary to note only that in 1537 he did not participate in the christening of his son, the future Edward VI.[41]

Although the next example of the misinterpretation of a religious ceremony does not apply to either Anne of Cleves or Anne Boleyn, it is important in further documenting recent modern confusion about early modern practices. Monarchs did not usually attend the last rites of passage for individuals of lesser social rank. Unaware of this custom, historians have speculated erroneously as to why James I was absent in 1619 from the funeral of his somewhat estranged wife, Anne of Denmark. He may well have been ill, and he seems to have harbored a "horror of death," as they suggest, but even had he been perfectly healthy and with no particular revulsion for mournful scenes, he still would not have been present at his wife's public services. Since heralds were in charge of conducting the death rituals of the reigning monarch, if custom had dictated James's attendance at the last public rites of his wife, the mother of his children and a representative of Denmark in England, he would have complied unless, of course, he had actually lain bedridden. Otherwise, his breach of protocol would have greatly offended members of the Danish royal family.[42]

To support this conclusion, it is possible to point to the absence of two Tudor monarchs from their wives' burial services, for which they have received no negative criticism in modern writings. Elizabeth of York's husband, Henry VII, who has often been characterized as financially shrewd, funded a lavish funeral for her. Despite this great expenditure, he was not present at her public rites in 1503 because, according to Michael van Cleave Alexander, who quoted a Tudor writer, the inconsolable king "Privily departed to a solitary place, and would no man should resort unto him."[43] In 1537 his namesake son, Henry VIII, deeply upset about the death of his wife Jane Seymour in childbirth, ordered Thomas Howard, third duke of Norfolk, and Sir William Paulet to arrange her burial, and then retired to a solitary place.[44]

Another death custom perplexing to modern historians is the condemned persons' expressions of their feelings in their final speeches. Many, such as the alleged lovers of Anne Boleyn, who were probably innocent of the specific crimes for which they were to suffer execution, nevertheless admitted their guilt, although mostly in a general sense.[45] They confessed for at least three reasons: the wish to protect their families from further punishment, the desire to obtain more merciful or quicker deaths, and the hope to facilitate their passage through purgatory. Since early modern Christians identified themselves as the heirs of Adam, whom God had expelled from paradise, they believed that they had inherited his sinful nature and were deserving of death. Even as they admitted their general guilt as human beings, they begged the king's forgiveness and remarked kindly about his character. This was the expected procedure. Whether the condemned actually felt that much remorse is another matter, but in the *ars moriendi* tradition, they were preparing for death in the hope of eternal bliss: One's final speech was not a time to settle earthly scores.[46]

Two other rituals concerning Henry VIII's family are also interesting. Henry absented himself, as expected, from the public celebration of Anne Boleyn's coronation in 1533 because of hierarchical considerations, but he actually performed a customary greeting ceremony for Anne of Cleves in 1540. While his expected absence from Anne Boleyn's coronation has caused little comment, since he was clearly still hoping his pregnant wife would be delivered of a live male child,[47] his incognito greeting of

Anne of Cleves has elicited many erroneous interpretations. To perform the ritual he and some members of his privy chamber had to travel in disguise from Greenwich to Rochester where Anne had only recently arrived on her journey from Cleves to Greenwich. When he first saw her at Rochester, he was disappointed with her appearance and later confessed to his attendants that she was not as "fair" as he had expected.[48]

Many writers subsequently interpreted this meeting as idiosyncratic, as something the old, lustful, and somewhat out-of-control king decided to do in his impatience to view his new, young wife. This is an entirely problematic analysis, for it was, in fact, a form of the greeting ritual that monarchs performed all across Christendom when they married foreign-born wives whom they had never met. Derived from the chivalric tradition of love at first sight, the ritual dictated the unannounced appearance of the groom in disguise, thus offering the bride an opportunity to fall in love with him as a man rather than as a powerful and rich king. Henry was not the first monarch to meet his new wife in disguise and he was not to be the last. In 1660 Louis XIV was probably the final performer of the ritual, for by the late seventeenth century much of the remaining chivalric culture of early modern society was disappearing, as it had increasingly become characterized as dated and old-fashioned.[49]

Before turning to the methodology used in my studies of Anne Boleyn and Anne of Cleves, I shall explain why they became the objects of my research. Although G. R. Elton was best known for favoring political history and for opposing biographical studies, cultural history, and social history, including family and gender studies, he actually recommended, when I first met him in the summer of 1984, that I compose a biography of Anne Boleyn. As he had recently read my book, *Women of the English Renaissance and Reformation*, published by Greenwood Press in 1983, he was aware, when he invited me to research the 1530s—the important Reformation decade he had dominated for more than thirty years—that my point of view differed from his. My analysis would necessarily integrate the political history of the court with other types of history. Embarking upon a study of Anne Boleyn was not on my agenda in 1984; I had planned to do a collaborative study of Jacobean funeral sermons for women with my colleague, Professor Bettie Anne Doebler of the English department at Arizona State University. Elton's suggestion, which I nevertheless accepted, changed the shape and scope of my future research. It ultimately became clear to me that by the time of our conversation in 1984, Elton had concluded that the interpretations of politics at Henry VIII's court were sterile and unhistorical, for he readily accepted my thesis about sexual heresy, which linked the charges against Anne Boleyn with witchcraft, and approved my suggestion that the mysterious events surrounding her death could best be explained by her probable miscarriage of a deformed fetus. While undertaking and completing the research on Anne Boleyn, I became interested in the erroneous use of rituals as evidence for the private beliefs of the Tudors. It was logical that when I finished her biography I should turn to Henry's greeting of Anne of Cleves at Rochester and then to a larger study of her life. [50]

Freeing the life stories of these two royal consorts from centuries-old tiers of bias and misinformation formed a significant part of my research. As I was gathering, questioning, and validating the evidence, I began to consider how I should conceptualize their lives. Since, as Ira Bruce Nadel has maintained, "how the biographer expresses the life becomes the real subject of the biography," this decision is an extremely important but often difficult one for authors to reach. [51] I searched for a framework that would at once highlight the women's significance and provide a structure for describing the facts of their lives. One major obstacle to an understanding of their characters was that neither Anne Boleyn nor Anne of Cleves left much information, at least that is extant, that might be called introspective. They kept no diaries or journals and only a few of their letters have survived. Unlike Anne Boleyn, Anne of Cleves did leave a will. I worried whether the evidence would be sufficient to enable me to conceptualize their lives and provide my audience with at least a hint of their personalities. Who were these women, I wondered, whom Henry had married and then so abruptly rejected?

I found the answer to this question in examining the evidence concerning their participation in the rites of passage, especially marriage and childbirth, and in their kinship and family relationships. To other scholars this choice might have appeared self-evident, since my subjects were born into a patriarchal society that socialized them to marry and have children.

From their early years, while they did not anticipate marrying a monarch, they expected to wed the heir of a noble house. The problem with this conceptualization was that it seemed to reduce their lives to their sexual and biological functions. Kathleen Berry later articulated this dilemma in an essay on the life of Susan B. Anthony when she said, "To define women by their sexuality and reproductivity is to remove them from the progression of history."[52] It is also true, however, as Carolyn Heilbrun has affirmed, that until the eighteenth century the two topics on which women could speak with some authority were those concerning family and religion.[53]

Earlier biographers viewed Anne Boleyn as a religious reformer, as a home wrecker, as a witch, and even as a courtly lover, but the bulk of the extant evidence did not seem to support those roles. As the title of my book indicates, I chose to place her life within the larger framework of her family ties and patronage relationships at court. So much information in the study processed the evidence of her networking with relatives and clients that I felt it necessary to deny in the preface that my work could be defined as a traditional biography.[54] In so doing, I accepted, without knowing it, the spirit of Richard Wortman's earlier statement in 1985 about Russian intelligentsia: "The experiences of the individual become historically meaningful to me only when they are set in the context of the experiences of others with similar concerns." He went on to explain, "I have approached biography as a way to comprehend history, to understand movements and currents of thought by examining the lives of individuals who contributed to them."[55] In other words, interpreting Anne Boleyn's life within her family and kinship network not only leads us to a fuller understanding of her as a person but also to a fuller understanding of the workings of politics at the Tudor court.

Far from viewing Anne Boleyn as a flirtatious, manipulative woman who single-handedly wrecked the king's first marriage, I saw her as an important player in family and kinship strategies. That the king eagerly courted her is irrefutable, for he expressed his love in seventeen extant letters to her. It seemed to me that once they were wed, she operated on the assumption that the political future of herself and her ambitious relatives depended on her ability to bear a healthy male heir. In that sense, her goal was to fulfill the traditional biological expectations of the crowned queen of England. No extant contemporary record dated before the events culminating in her death in May 1536 indicated that as queen she had acted promiscuously or flirtatiously. Not a hint or rumor of this behavior appeared in Chapuys's dispatches. Even the letters her jailer at the Tower wrote detailing her confessions indicated that she admitted only to having rejected the unsolicited flattery of two of the alleged lovers. That denial has ironically surfaced as the prime evidence for claiming she was too flirtatious for her own good, for her own self-preservation.[56]

My biography of Anne of Cleves, in contrast with other modern accounts, focuses not so much on her ties to her relatives, although they played an important role in the arranging of her marriage, as on the marital process itself. In an important sense, her life is a microcosm of the history of early modern brides who were expected to travel to foreign, sometimes hostile, countries, where they often did not understand the language of their new husbands, as Anne of Cleves did not, and where they were expected to become accustomed to unfamiliar daily practices and mores, from dining habits to religious observances. Because the life of Anne of Cleves, like that of Anne Boleyn, takes into account the larger picture, I indicated in the introduction that my study of her was not a traditional biography either.[57]

When the king ordered her removal from court as the first step in achieving an annulment of their union, she compared her plight to that of the rusticated Catherine of Aragon, his first wife, and during the remaining seven years of the king's life, she yearned to return to her position as his consort. She could realistically hope for a reconciliation because Church tradition blamed another person's witchcraft, rather than Anne's appearance, for the king's incapacity, which is defined as relative impotency when it is directed toward one specific woman, as his was toward her. Far from living contentedly as his rich sister, she suffered from deep humiliation and fell into great despair. A letter she wrote to her brother William, duke of Cleves, during the reign of her stepson, Edward VI, makes it clear that she was homesick. In the letter she complained that England was not her country and that she was a stranger there. Financial difficulties plagued her last years partly because of inflation and partly because of the decisions of Edward's privy council to confiscate some of her property.[58]

Biographers have traditionally relied on three basic types of structures for presenting the events of a person's life: chronological; topical; and "mixed media,"[59] Milton Lomask's term for a method that involves adopting a topical approach that moves forward by starts and stops in an overall chronological fashion. Because the entries I have submitted to encyclopedias, including several for the *New Dictionary of Biography*, have necessarily been limited in length and have usually had to fit predetermined editorial designs, I sometimes adopted a chronological structure in writing them. Yet I became concerned that using this method for a more detailed, book-length study could confuse readers. Basically, I support Lomask's conclusion that the "mixed media" approach seems to work best for these biographies because it provides space for contextual analysis but also shows a respect for the reading audience who expect a narrative that ultimately moves forward through time. Since I planned to center the lives of Anne Boleyn and Anne of Cleves within a larger family and marital context, the "mixed media" method seemed to offer me a valid and reliable means of presenting my material. It is an approach that is more clearly evident in the Anne of Cleves work than in the Anne Boleyn study; both, however, refer to all the biographical information that is known about them. I have never attempted the third method, that of recounting the subject's life using only topical chapters.[60]

As I explained in the discussion of why I embarked on a study of Anne Boleyn and Anne of Cleves, my point of view differs from that of their earlier biographers.[61] My method was to push aside the historical fictions on which their stories have been constructed to arrive, as much as possible, at the "truth" to which Robin Winks referred. Then I sought to provide the "justice" about which Garrett Mattingly wrote. My ultimate objective was to restore the women, to the extent it was possible given the nature of the evidence, to the place that they actually held in the political hierarchy of the court and their society.[62]

The decision to connect their lives to their family networks and their culture's marrying practices has played a large role in preventing one of the biographer's frequent pitfalls, that of having identified so closely with the subject as to lose objectivity.[63] While family considerations are important to modern professional women, our education, energy, drive, and intellectual and spiritual aspirations include so much more. Many of us have juggled careers and family responsibilities. Thus, while I learned to respect my two subjects, I can unhesitatingly state that I did not and do not now identify with them, nor do I yearn for a return of their society.[64] Although I do also respect Tudor culture, as a modern woman I feel somewhat estranged from the prescientific world in which churchmen, who reigned as experts on the laws of human reproduction, blamed witches for the birth of deformed infants and for the infliction of some forms of male impotency.

It is perhaps this very estrangement or aloofness from their culture, however, that has led me to feel great sympathy for them as women. Ironically, at the beginning of my studies of them, I did not expect this sympathy to develop, at least to the degree that it has. The reason for this skepticism is simply that, like earlier writers, I had absorbed the lore that Anne Boleyn was a somewhat disfigured but attractive woman who suffered death because of her flirtatious ways and that Anne of Cleves was a somewhat plain woman who welcomed forced retirement from a powerful and splendid Renaissance court. Instead, I learned from my research that these views had more in common with their earlier biographers' fantasies than with the facts of their existence. Both women had failed as Henry's consorts because of premodern ignorance concerning human sexuality and marriage. Their real histories were poignant and tragic, and the "truth" of them needs to replace the ubiquitous fictional accounts. In fact, this reshaping makes for a more interesting, believable story than the received tradition.

The precarious nature of Tudor history in academia, especially in the United States, also compels us to seek to provide "justice" in our studies of women. For the most part, established scholars who are teaching doctoral students about Tudor history are not in the United States but in England; the University of Nebraska–Lincoln is one of only a handful of major American universities with a Tudor specialist. The decrease in faculty teaching early modern English, not just Tudor, history here is a problem that Robert Tittler addressed in a recent article in *Albion*. In it, he also reported on the "highly specialized" and distinctive subfields of history in England where, for example, social history (including women's and gender) forms a distinct subfield from that of political history or religious history. Faculty in subfields attend their own conferences. According to Tittler, "at least figuratively speaking, there is certainly a tendency for members of each group to adjourn" to different "pubs" when their sessions are over. The university history departments in England reflect this specialization, which, as Tittler claimed, does not "preclude integration" but does not "facilitate" it either.[65]

What I am calling for, and what I hope others will undertake, is the integration of social and cultural history with political history, especially in Tudor biographies. Without making reference to advances in women's history, the history of sexuality, or family history, some biographers have ironically still attempted to write about individuals who lived in a society in which a personal monarch and his quest to sire male heirs were at the core of domestic and even international events. David Potter has even recently pointed out that in sixteenth-century Europe, "The game of marriage negotiations and alliances seemed to make the international system a vast family concern."[66]

To persuade others of the urgency of this integration is a necessary but difficult task, given the fractionalized history departments in England and the decayed state of Tudor academic history here.[67] Another important hindrance to change is the staying power of traditional views. After the more than four hundred years that have elapsed since these legends about Anne Boleyn and Anne of Cleves began to take root, the accepted interpretations of their lives so depend upon the fictions that some academic historians resist being deprived of them. Lomask pointed out in 1986, for example, that scholars have long known that Patrick Henry did not say, "If this be treason, make the most of it." Although the patriot's first biographer actually invented this speech, it has remained a part of the received wisdom of American history,[68] just as Anne Boleyn as a disfigured but flirtatious woman and Anne of Cleves as the unattractive but contented ex-wife have remained a part of the received wisdom of English history.

Reshaping the lives of Tudor women, despite the troublesome nature of the evidence about them in both primary and secondary works and the existence of other obstacles, is an important part of the ongoing process of recovering the history of Englishwomen through a sensitive evaluation of the issues that most directly affected them. A knowledge of new research on the history of sexuality and family history will, furthermore, enable scholars who wish to undertake a study of Englishwomen's lives to eliminate the negative gendered attitudes that still prevail in some modern studies. A greater sensitivity to the limitations that past hierarchical and patriarchal societies imposed upon Englishwomen will further enhance our appreciation of their experiences. Ultimately, if we are to achieve a fuller understanding of the history of society as a whole, of both men and women, this is a necessary endeavor, a challenge that we must and should accept.

Notes

1. Sara Mendelson and Patricia Crawford, *Women in Early Modern England*, 1550–1720 (Oxford: Oxford University Press, 1998), 1.

2. A. N. McLaren, *Political Culture in the Reign of Elizabeth I: Queen and Commonwealth*, 1558–1585 (Cambridge: Cambridge University Press, 1999).

3. Robin Winks, *The Historian as Detective: Essays on Evidence* (New York: Harper & Row, 1968), 229.

4. Ira Bruce Nadel, *Biography: Fiction, Fact, and Form* (London: Macmillan, 1984), 6.

5. Christopher Parker, *The English Historical Tradition since 1850* (Edinburgh: John Donald, 1990), 88–91.

6. Anne-Katherine Broch-Due, "Reflections on Subjectivism in Biographical Interviewing: A Process of Change," in *All Sides of the Subject: Women and Biography*, ed. Teresa Iles (New York: Teachers College Press, 1992), 93.

7. For a brief overview of biographical writing, see Catherine N. Parke, *Biography: Writing Lives* (New York: Twayne, 1996), 1–34; and, for example, A. F. Pollard, *Henry VIII* (New York: Longman, Greens, 1902).

8. Paul M. Kendall, *The Art of Biography* (New York: W. W. Norton, 1965), 3–4.

9. Sir John Neale, *Queen Elizabeth* (New York: Harcourt, Brace, 1934).

10. He said this so often in public settings that it does not need a citation.

11. Samuel H. Baron, "Psychological Dimensions of the Biographical Process," in *Introspection in Biography: The Biographer's Quest for Self-Awareness*, ed. Baron and

Carl Pletsch (Hillsdale NJ: Analytic Press, 1985), 1; Parke, *Biography*, xv, reports that in public libraries biography stacks are located next to fiction, a placement that signals the libraries' recognition of their popularity; Stephen B. Oates, ed., "Introduction," in *Biography as High Adventure: Life-Writers Speak on Their Art* (Amherst: University of Massachusetts Press, 1986), ix, reports that biographical titles have doubled since the 1960s.

    12. Retha M. Warnicke, "The Conventions of Courtly Love and Anne Boleyn," in *State, Sovereigns and Society in Early Modern England*, ed. Charles Carlton (Thrupp, England: Sutton, 1998), 103–18.

    13. Garrett Mattingly, *The Armada* (Boston: Houghton Mifflin, 1959), 375.

    14. Winks, *Historian as Detective*, xiv.

    15. *The Acts and Monuments of John Foxe*, ed. George Townsend, 8 vols. (1837–41; reprint, New York: AMS Press, 1965), 5:136.

    16. J. H. Plumb, "The Private Grief of Public Figures," *Biography and Truth*, ed. Stanley Wientraub (Indianapolis: The Bobbs-Merrill Co., 1967), 12–14.

    17. Warnicke, *The Rise and Fall of Anne Boleyn: Family Politics at the Court of Henry VIII* (Cambridge: Cambridge University Press, 1989), 191–233. For a survey of the historical caricatures of Henry VIII, see Esme Wingfield-Stratford, *Truth in Masquerade: A Study of Fashions in Fact* (New York: Roy Publisher, 1951), 100–118.

    18. *Acts and Monuments of Foxe*, vol. 8.

    19. A. G. Dickens, *The English Reformation* (New York: Schocken Books, 1964), 108.

    20. Dickens, *English Reformation*, 108.

    21. Both resided at schismatic courts and were probably antipapal, but no evidence exists that they otherwise doubted the validity of the seven sacraments of the Holy Roman Catholic Church. Warnicke, *Anne Boleyn*, 151–62; Warnicke, *The Marrying of Anne of Cleves: Royal Protocol in Tudor England* (Cambridge: Cambridge University Press, 2000), 63–93.

    22. James A. Froude, *History of England from the Fall of Wolsey to the Death of Elizabeth* (New York: C. Scribner's Sons, 1870), 8:67, 74, 134–147.

    23. Warnicke, *Anne of Cleves*, 216.

    24. See also Natalie Z. Davis, *Fiction in the Archives: Pardon Tales and Other Tellers in Sixteenth-Century France* (Stanford: Stanford University Press, 1987).

    25. W. C. Richardson, *Mary Tudor: The White Queen* (London: Peter Owen, 1970), 3.

    26. Warnicke, *Anne Boleyn*, 8–10; Lacey B. Smith, *A Tudor Tragedy: The Life and*

Times of Catherine Howard (New York: Pantheon, 1961), 209–11. For Christina, see Warnicke, *Anne of Cleves*, 40–43.

27. Warnicke, *Anne of Cleves*, 12–35.

28. Warnicke, *Anne Boleyn*, 1–3, 104, 114.

29. Paul Friedmann, *Anne Boleyn: A Chapter of English History, 1527–1536* (London: Macmillan, 1884), 1:viii. For a modern history that relies on Chapuys, see E. W. Ives, *Anne Boleyn* (Oxford: Basil Blackwell, 1986).

30. Malcolm Gaskill, "Reporting Murder: Fiction in the Archives in Early Modern England," *Social History* 22 (1998): 1–30. See also Gaskill, *Crime and Mentalities in Early Modern England* (Cambridge: Cambridge University Press, 2000).

31. Warnicke, *Anne Boleyn*, 215.

32. Warnicke, *Anne of Cleves*, 155–86.

33. Retha M. Warnicke, "Three Forged Letters of Anne Boleyn: Their Implications for Reformation Politics and Women's Studies," *Journal of the Rocky Mountain Medieval and Renaissance Association* 11(1990): 33–48.

34. Warnicke, "Three Forged Letters of Anne Boleyn," 33–48; Froude, *History of England*, 2:463–66.

35. Retha M. Warnicke, "Lady Mildmay's Journal: A Study in Autobiography and Meditation in Reformation England," *Sixteenth Century Journal* 20 (1989): 55–68.

36. B. A. Lees, "The Letters of Eleanor of Aquitaine to Celestine III," *English Historical Review* 21 (1906): 78–93.

37. Warnicke, *Anne Boleyn*, 243–47; Warnicke, "More's Richard III and the Mystery Plays," *Historical Journal* 35 (1992): 761–78; Warnicke, "The Physical Deformities of Anne Boleyn and Richard III: Myth and Reality," *Paragon*, n.s., 4 (1986): 135–53; Warnicke, "Conflicting Rhetoric about Tudor Women: The Example of Queen Anne Boleyn," *The Rhetoric of Politics and Renaissance Women*, ed. Carole Levin and Patricia Sullivan (Albany: State University of New York Press, 1995), 39–56.

38. Warnicke, *Anne of Cleves*, 86–93, 256, 265.

39. Warnicke, *Anne of Cleves*, 259; Alison Weir, *The Six Wives of Henry VIII* (New York: Grove Weidenfeld, 1991), 396; Ives, *Anne Boleyn*, 4–52; Warnicke, *Anne Boleyn*, 243–47.

40. Winks, *Historian as Detective*, 229.

41. Warnicke, *Anne Boleyn*, 169–70.

42. For example, David Willson, *King James VI and I* (New York: Oxford University Press, 1967), 403–4.

43. Michael van Cleave Alexander, *The First of the Tudors: A Study of Henry VII and His Reign* (Totowa NJ: Rowman & Littlefield, 1980), 185.

44. *Letters and Papers, Foreign and Domestic of the Reign of Henry VIII*, ed. J. S. Brewer, J. Gairdner, and R. H. Brodie (London: Her Majesty's Stationery Office, 1862–1932), 8:ii, #1060.

45. Froude, *History of England*, 2:482–87.

46. K. Jankofsky, "Public Executions in England in the Late Middle Ages: The Indignity and Dignity of Death," *Omega: Journal of Death and Dying* 10 (1979): 43–4; Lacey B. Smith, "English Treason Trials and Confessions in the Sixteenth Century," *Journal of the History of Ideas* 15 (1954): 482; Warnicke, *Anne Boleyn*, 232, 303, n. 57.

47. Warnicke, *Anne Boleyn*, 124–30.

48. Warnicke, *Anne of Cleves*, 127–35; idem, "Henry VIII's greeting of Anne of Cleves, and Early Modern Protocol," *Albion* 28 (1996): 565–86.

49. Warnicke, *Anne of Cleves*, 135–36.

50. For a discussions of how biographers choose their topics see Baron, "Introduction," *Introspection in Biography*, 3.

51. Craig Kridel, ed., "Introduction," *Writing Educational Biography: Explorations in Qualitative Research* (New York: Garland, 1998), 94; Nadel, *Biography*, 154.

52. Kathleen Berry, "Toward a Theory of Women's Biography: From the Life of Susan B. Anthony," *Women and Biography*, 28.

53. Carolyn G. Heilbrun, *Writing a Woman's Life* (New York: W. W. Norton, 1988), 25.

54. Warnicke, *Anne Boleyn*, ix.

55. Richard Wortman, "Biography and the Russian Intelligentsia," in *Introspection in Biography*, 157.

56. Ives, *Anne Boleyn*, 374.

57. Warnicke, *Anne of Cleves*, 11.

58. Warnicke, *Anne of Cleves*, 184–86, 229–57. Actually, one of the official grounds for divorce was that she was already married to the heir of Lorraine. Documentation that Henry VIII did not possess proves that she was not. She and her Cleves contemporaries were all in agreement on this point.

59. Milton Lomask, *The Biographer's Craft* (New York: Harper & Row, 1986), 41.

60. Maria Dowling, *Fisher of Men: A Life of John Fisher, 1469–1535* (London: MacMillan, 1999), 4–6, has not entirely successfully used this method. She tried to compensate for the difficulty with her presentation by giving her readers a short synopsis of his life in the Introduction.

61. Nadel, *Biography*, 7, 103, discusses a point of view.

62. Winks, *Historian as Detective*, xiv; Mattingly, *Armada*, 375.

63. John A. Garraty, *The Nature of Biography* (New York: Alfred A. Knopf, 1957), 28.

64. Liz Stanley, "Process in Feminist Biography and Feminist Epistemology," *Women and Biography*, 109.

65. Robert Tittler, "Early Modern British History, Here and There, Now and Again," *Albion* 32 (1999): 190–206.

66. David Potter, *A History of France. 1460–1560: The Emergence of a Nation State* (London: Macmillan, 1995), 257.

67. John Guy, editor of the Early Modern Series at Cambridge University Press and professor at St. Andrew's, has been extremely helpful and supportive of this integrative process.

68. Lomask, *Biographer's Craft*, 35.

Selected Bibliography

Baron, Samuel H., and Carol Pletsch, eds. *Introspection in Biography: The Biographer's Quest for Self-Awareness.* Hillsdale NJ: Analytic Press, 1985.

Davis, Natalie Z. *Fiction in the Archives: Pardon Tales and Other Tellers in Sixteenth-Century France.* Stanford CA: Stanford University Press, 1987.

Friedmann, Paul. *Anne Boleyn: A Chapter of English History, 1527–1536.* 2 vols. London: Macmillan, 1884.

Heilbrun, Carolyn G. *Writing a Woman's Life.* New York: W. W. Norton, 1988.

Iles, Teresa, ed. *All Sides of the Subject: Women and Biography.* New York: Teachers College Press, 1992.

Ives, E. W. *Anne Boleyn.* Oxford: Basil Blackwell, 1986.

Kridel, Craig, ed. *Writing Educational Biography: Explorations in Qualitative Research.* New York: Garland, 1998.

McClaren, A. N. *Political Culture in the Reign of Elizabeth I: Queen and Commonwealth, 1558–1585.* Cambridge: Cambridge University Press, 1999.

Mendelson, Sara, and Patricia Crawford. *Women in Early Modern England: 1550–1720.* Oxford: Oxford University Press, 1998.

Nadel, Ira Bruce. *Biography: Fiction, Fact, and Form.* London: Macmillan, 1984.

Neale, John. *Queen Elizabeth.* New York: Harcourt, Brace, 1934.

Oates, Stephen B. ed. *Biography as High Adventure: Life-Writers Speak on Their Art.* Amherst: University of Massachusetts Press, 1986.

Parke, Catherine N. *Biography: Writing Lives.* New York: Twayne, 1996.

Pollard, A. F. *Henry VIII*. New York: Longman, Greens, 1902.

Richardson, W. C. *Mary Tudor: The White Queen*. London: Peter Owen, 1970.

Van Cleve Alexander, Michael. *The First of the Tudors: A Study of Henry VIII and His Reign*. Totowa NJ: Rowman & Littlefield, 1980.

Warnicke, Retha M. *The Marrying of Anne of Cleves: Royal Protocol in Tudor England*. Cambridge: Cambridge University Press, 2000.

———. *The Rise and Fall of Anne Boleyn: Family Politics at the Court of Henry VIII*. Cambridge: Cambridge University Press, 1989.

———. "Conflicting Rhetoric about Tudor Women: The Example of Queen Anne Boleyn." *The Rhetoric of Politics and Renaissance Women*, 39–56. Edited by Carole Levin and Patricia Sullivan. Albany: State University of New York Press, 1995.

———. "The Conventions of Courtly Love and Anne Boleyn." *State, Sovereigns and Society in Early Modern England*, 103–18. Edited by Charles Carlton. Thrupp, England: Sutton, 1998.

———. "The Physical Deformities of Anne Boleyn and Richard III: Myth and Reality." *Paragon* n.s., 5 (1986): 135–53.

———. "Three Forged Letters of Anne Boleyn: Their Implications for Reformation Politics and Women's Studies." *Journal of the Rocky Mountain Medieval and Renaissance Association* 11 (1990): 33–48.

Weintraub, Stanley, ed. *Biography and Truth*. Indianapolis: Bobbs-Merrill, 1967.

Winks, Robin. *The Historian as Detective: Essays on Evidence*. New York: Harper & Row, 1968.

4. Conception, Conversation, and Comparison: My Experiences as a Biographer

John Milton Cooper Jr.

My experience as a biographer has taught me one big lesson: There's no substitute for experience. I think that biography is like sports or music or drama. You can enjoy it a lot from a seat in the stadium or the theater. You can also learn a lot about it by reading and hearing the reflections of biographers. But if you really want to be a biographer, you should skip this chapter and get back to your research and writing. If you choose to stick around, I shall try to compensate you for being away from your real work by passing along some other lessons that I have learned in my limited experiences at the biographer's trade.

Before I get to those lessons, let me give you a quick account of what I have done in the way of biography. My experience really started in college. Princeton required a senior thesis, and I had to come up with a topic. I chose the Illinois senator and political associate of Abraham Lincoln—Lyman Trumbull. Trumbull was one of the fabled "Seven Martyrs"—the Republicans who voted against Andrew Johnson's conviction in 1868 and supplied the one-third plus one needed to save him from removal from office. I wasn't foolish enough to try to tackle Trumbull's whole life or career. I restricted myself to his participation in Reconstruction. This was a great experience for me. My adviser was a leading Civil War historian; I learned a lot from him and even more from my own efforts. Undertaking this study helped push me down the road toward becoming a professional historian.

My next experience was similar. In graduate school I had to write a master's thesis. I was already interested in foreign policy, and I wanted to knock off this thesis with dispatch. Therefore, I used what I had learned about the era of Reconstruction to write about Charles Sumner's role in blocking the Grant administration's attempt to annex Santo Domingo. This was also a good experience, but, as I said, I regarded this as a means to an end.

The end was to get on to twentieth-century political history, especially as it affected foreign policy. Since there have been many persons who have played great roles in that arena, I could have stuck with biography. As a matter of fact, my first published article was a speculative biographical essay about a great isolationist, Senator William E. Borah of Idaho. But for my dissertation I forsook biography to study isolationism itself. That dissertation became my first book.[1]

For my second book, it was back to biography. My subject was Walter Hines Page. I shall say more about him and about this book when I get into the three aspects of writing biography. All I want to say about Page now is that he was good company over the several years that I spent with him, and he confirmed me in my taste for biography.[2]

My next book and thus far only other published biography was different. It belongs to a rare genre: comparative biography. In this case, the subjects I was comparing were Theodore Roosevelt and Woodrow Wilson. This was also a most enjoyable and stimulating experience.[3]

Those reflect nearly all of my experiences as a biographer. I have not done a book-length biography since the comparative one on Roosevelt and Wilson, but I do plan to get back into the trenches quite soon.

Now, let me turn to the three "c" words that make up the title of this chapter—conception, conversation, and comparison. I want to discuss each one in light of what people in the eighteenth century called "the lamp of experience."

By conception, I do not mean the formation of interpretative concepts, although that is an important aspect of biography. What I mean here is how biographers choose their subjects. From my reading of biographers on biography, this is something that they tend to pass over quickly as if it holds little interest.

The one great exception to this omission whom I have encountered is Catherine Drinker Bowen. In some of her essays on biography, Bowen talks quite a bit about how she selected her subjects. One thing that I particularly remember from those essays is that Bowen says she did not want to write about someone who died comparatively young. She wanted to write about people who lived to an old age. She does not discuss why she never chose a woman as her subject, but, to be fair to Bowen, she does compensate for that neglect of her own gender in her extensive treatment of Abigail Adams in her biography of John Adams. She also gives more than equal time to the female members of her family in her magnificent memoir, Family Portrait.[4]

Otherwise, biographers tend to say little about how they choose their subjects. Let me try to compensate for their silence with a few reflections from my own experience. Let me also say at the outset that I am talking from the viewpoint of a professional, academic historian. There are many reasons that people choose their subjects and write their biographies. For me and my academic ilk, however, there is always the requirement that our subjects have historical significance and that they illuminate important things about the times in which they lived and the events in which they participated. This is the historian's equivalent of the literary biographer's need to choose a subject who meets standards of aesthetic and cultural significance.

For historians who are biographers, there is also the requirement that sufficient material exist for an examination of their subjects' lives. Such materials usually mean manuscript sources — preferably a substantial body of the subject's diaries, letters, and other private writings. This is not always the case. From my own field, I can think of four examples in which historian-biographers had to overcome the handicap of lacking their subjects' personal papers. The first example is Stanley Coben, who wrote about the attorney general who mounted the Red Scare in 1919 and 1920 — A. Mitchell Palmer. As Coben pointed out, Palmer was an unlikely candidate for the role of red-baiter-in-chief at the end of World War I. He had previously been a progressive reformer with strong ties to organized labor and social justice groups. What is more, he was by birth and upbringing a Quaker. In Palmer, Coben found what is a rare and interesting phenomenon, what he called a "liberal demagogue."[5]

The second example is William Holmes, who wrote a biography of another demagogue. His subject was the flamboyant Mississippi governor and senator who combined advanced reformist stands on the leading economic and social issues of the day with virulent white racism—James K. Vardaman. Better than anyone else, I think, Vardaman personified what C. Vann Woodward once called "progressivism for whites only." Indeed, in Vardaman's case this went further to embody progressivism for whites at the expense of the active and self-conscious degradation of African Americans. Vardaman was not just a demagogue who used racist appeals to get himself elected. In office he delivered on his campaign promises to make life even more restricted and miserable than it already was for African Americans.[6]

The third example is David Levy, who wrote a biography of someone who ranks as one of the greatest, even perhaps the greatest, political intellectuals of twentieth-century America—Herbert Croly. Croly wrote a book, *The Promise of American Life*, that ranks alongside Alexis de Tocqueville's *Democracy in America* and W. E. B. DuBois's *Souls of Black Folk* in its brilliant and deep insights into the life of this nation. Croly was also the founding editor of the *New Republic*, which, under his editorship, George Kennan has called the greatest magazine ever published in America. Croly assembled a veritable galaxy of intellectual and literary stars, including his fellow editor Walter Lippmann and such regular contributors as Charles Beard, Randolph Bourne, Robert Frost, and Rebecca West, to name a few.[7]

My final example is T. Harry Williams, who wrote on the magisterial life of Huey Long. Does this subject need any introduction from me? I don't think so, except to say that probably no politician in twentieth-century America dominated his state as thoroughly as Long did Louisiana, or cast so long and deep a shadow over politics there after his death. Furthermore, Huey Long ranks alongside Eugene Debs and Robert La Follette as one of the most effective radical leaders in twentieth-century America.[8]

How did these three historian-biographers overcome their subjects' lack of personal papers? They did it in three ways. First, they combed other manuscript collections of these men's contemporaries to find material from and about them. Second, they combed the public record for material by and about them. In the cases of Palmer, Vardaman, and Long, the subjects were in public life, gave a lot of speeches, and were written about widely in the press. In Vardaman's case, the *Congressional Record* was especially valuable. In Croly's case, there were his own fairly extensive published writings. Using such public records may seem obvious, but you would be surprised how historian-biographers, with their fetish for manuscript research, tend to neglect these records.

The third way in which these biographers overcame the lack of personal papers was through seeking out living people who knew and remembered their subjects. This is usually called "oral history." Each of these biographers was able to get in just ahead of the grim reaper and talk to their subjects' surviving associates and family members.

Most historian-biographers would not dare to approach a subject who lacked personal papers. These four persons did because their subjects were so significant and so central to their times. Most historians shy away from such persons, and rightly so. Even with subjects like Palmer, Vardaman, Croly, and Long there is still that sense of something missing, something that you wish you could see and know.

Now, let me get personal and tell you how I came to choose my subjects. On the matter of historical significance and illumination of one's times, I acted like a good academic plugged in to the current concerns within the profession. That was even true when I was a college senior. The time was the early 1960s. I don't think the term "second reconstruction" had come into use yet, but the idea of gaining knowledge of the present from the past was in the air. My subject, Trumbull, attracted me because he represented what seemed to be a forgotten middle ground. He was sometimes called a radical Republican, yet he balked at tossing Johnson out of office. My master's thesis reflected the same sort of concerns. Sumner ranked with Thaddeus Stevens as the quintessential radical, and his interest in foreign policy was unusual at that time.

By the time I came to select subjects for my two biographical books I was much better initiated into academic concerns, and I could justify Page and Roosevelt and Wilson on sound scholarly grounds. Page promised to illuminate a number of major themes of the time. He was a reform-minded white Southerner of the progressive era but a far more appealing figure than Vardaman. He was not a paragon of racial enlightenment by any stretch of the imagination, but he did embody what passed then for moderation and a sympathetic attitude toward African Americans. As a magazine editor, he published articles by Du Bois, and as a book publisher he encouraged and published both Charles W. Chesnut and Booker T. Washington. He became a friend of the Wizard of Tuskegee through his efforts to promote educational, economic, and public health progress in the South. For the sake of full disclosure, however, I have to point out that Page was also a friend and publisher of Thomas Dixon. He came to regret his role in fostering Dixon's literary career after he saw the motion picture *Birth of a Nation*, which was based on one of Dixon's novels that Page had published.

Of equally great scholarly concern to me was Page's association with Woodrow Wilson. The two men had known each other since they were in their twenties, when neither one had yet embarked on his main career. Page was one of the first people to tout Wilson for president after his election as governor of New Jersey. He was such an intimate of Wilson's that he barely missed appointment to two cabinet spots, and he happily settled for the consolation prize of ambassador to Great Britain. That appointment put him in the thick of American foreign policy during World War I. Insofar as Page is remembered today, it is mainly for that brief, intense, final diplomatic phase of his career. When people asked me who he was, my shorthand answer was "Woodrow Wilson's ambassador to Britain."

Likewise, in selecting him as a subject, I carefully weighed the questions of private materials and their accessibility. This was what we today call a no-brainer. I was teaching at Wellesley when I started to weigh my first post-dissertation project. The two major figures of the Wilson circle who had not had biographies done since the 1930s were Page and Edward M. House. The Texas colonel would have been a good subject. He was indisputably significant for his closeness to Wilson, and his voluminous, revealing diaries and papers were nearby, at Yale. I decided against House when I learned that a very good historian of about my age had already embarked on a biography of him. There were no competitors for Page, however, and his papers were even closer to hand, at the Houghton Library at Harvard, only a subway ride away. I must admit that another attraction was that working on Page's diplomatic phase would supply a professional excuse for spending time in England.

After I finished the Page biography, the book on Roosevelt and Wilson seemed like a natural progression. I had just finished writing about an important secondary figure of this era. Why not now tackle the two giants of the time? Believe me, it is hard to work in the political and diplomatic history of the first two decades of the twentieth century and not be drawn to those two men. They are the twin flames that lure historian-moths like me.

Significance presented no problem. Unquestionably, Roosevelt and Wilson dominated those decades like twin colossi. These two engaged in fierce rivalry and debate in a way that engaged the major domestic and foreign policy issues of their time. First, they had run against each other for president in 1912, each with a great slogan and argument, Roosevelt's "New Nationalism" versus Wilson's "New Freedom." Their arguments had delved into the major strains of American politics for most of the succeeding century. Moreover, their conflict over America's posture toward World War I had come at a critical, formative moment in both this nation's foreign policy and in world politics. In all, the richness, depth, and timing of their conflict and debate made them look to me like twentieth-century analogues to Alexander Hamilton and Thomas Jefferson.

Most historian-biographers would probably stop with those considerations. Such concerns about significance and illumination do constitute the main reasons that most of my breed choose the subjects they do. But I would be misleading you if I stopped here. These considerations weighed heavily on me, but they are not the only reasons that I chose these subjects. For me, there has also always been an irrational attraction that played a role in three of my choices. In the case of my college thesis and the two books, there was an experience that planted the seed that later grew into the biography.

Each experience was a moment of sheer, cussed interest in the person and persons for no particular reason. With Lyman Trumbull, it started with his name. It stuck in my head when I read Allan Nevins's *Ordeal of the Union* in a class on the Civil War era. Then I repeatedly encountered him, first as one of the maverick Republicans in the Johnson trial, next as an 1872 Liberal Republican, and finally, near the end of his life, as a Populist and legal mentor to Clarence Darrow.

With Page, I can remember the first time that I ever heard of him. As a college senior, while I was waiting for a class section to begin in the office of my favorite professor (an English, not a history, professor) I picked a book off his shelf. It was *The Training of an American: The Earlier Life and Letters of Walter Hines Page* by Burton J. Hendrick. Later, in graduate school, I encountered Page as a full-throated imperialist in 1898, and then, when I worked with the Wilson papers for my dissertation, I kept encountering his letters as ambassador. These epistles stood out for several reasons. They were much longer than almost anything that passed across the president's desk. Moreover, although most people's correspondence was typewritten, these letters were written in a clear, beautiful handwriting that even then usually came from the pens of only professional calligraphers. Finally, also unlike most of the letters Wilson received, these were not restrained, balanced statements of pros and cons of policy. They were unabashed pleas for the United States to back the Allies, especially Britain, in the war. The only element of restraint in these letters was the muted criticism of Wilson's policies, which Page vented in his sporadically kept diaries. I kept wondering, who was this guy? Where did he get off writing to the president like that?[9]

Likewise, with Roosevelt and Wilson, I can remember exactly when the thought of comparing them first crossed my mind. It was when I first read these two sentences in Robert Osgood's great book *Ideals and Self-Interest in America's Foreign Relations*: "In some respects, Roosevelt comes into sharpest focus when he is placed opposite Wilson, for there was something elemental in his antipathy for that good gentleman. One is reminded of Nietzsche's distinction between the Warrior and the Priest." Those sentences fascinated me in part because of the time and place at which I read them. It was 1964 and I was a graduate student at Columbia, just starting my dissertation. For more than a decade before, questions about the relationship of intellectuals to power had been rife, especially among New York's literati and scholars. Frankly, the way those folks asked and answered questions bothered me. They argued over intellectuals' "alienation" from power, and, despite their being smitten with Adlai Stevenson and John Kennedy, they usually came down on the side of exalting such alienation as the only proper stance toward power.[10]

Theodore Roosevelt and Woodrow Wilson struck me as outstanding counterexamples to those views. Here were two persons who were intellectuals as well as seekers after and wielders of power. Moreover, they believed that they could pursue both callings with little or no friction, much less contradiction. The invocation of Nietzsche's figures seemed to me to differentiate them perfectly. That loose term "intellectual," I thought, covered two distinct types—the artist on one side and the scholar or scientist on the other. Roosevelt appeared to me an artist whose medium was political power, someone who used ideas and concepts to inform and refine the practice of his art. Wilson struck me as the scholar whose medium was also political power, someone who used power to implement his ideas and ideals.

Why, you may ask, do I mention that interpretation now, as part of the personal fascination? Doesn't this fit the category of scholarly inspiration that often animates historian-biographers when they choose subjects? Isn't this an example of conception in the other sense, that is, the intellectual concepts that a scholar brings to the subject? In one way, it is, but it fits into my experience differently. Perhaps if I had run with those concepts right away and done a scholarly article or book rather quickly I would have stuck with those concepts. Fortunately for me, well over a decade and two books intervened before I began work on the book on Roosevelt and Wilson.

I say fortunately because the kind of conception for a biographer that I am talking about saved me from the hazards of the other kind of conception—namely, having preconceived notions and thereby making a biography, or any other work of history, a self-fulfilling prophecy. One of the things that neither historians nor biographers talk much about is the need to surrender themselves in some measure to their subjects. We need to retain the capacity for surprise and the willingness to follow our subjects down paths that we did not foresee or even down paths that take us in the opposite direction from the one in which we originally intended to go.

Let me illustrate what I mean with examples from my work on Page, Roosevelt, and Wilson. With Page, my first salutary surprise was that he had had a life before he became ambassador—a rich and varied life that came to interest me at least as much as his wartime diplomatic stint. Thanks to abundant sources about his earlier years, I found myself exposed to subjects that had seldom crossed my mind before. One was the history of magazines and book publishing, especially the managerial and business sides of those fields. Another was the phenomenon of the white Southern expatriate after the Civil War. Such expatriates as Page and Wilson, too, retained strong ties to their native region. Both this phenomenon and Page's embodiment of it struck personal chords with me because my parents came from his native state, North Carolina, and were themselves expatriates.

For me, the greatest surprise with Page came in an entirely unexpected area, that of gender history. In those days, the term "gender" was rarely used in historical writing, and women's history was still in its infancy. Looking back on my experience, I realize how much I was stumbling in the dark. What I found in Page was a gendered domestic drama that was not supposed to happen in a place like rural North Carolina at the time of the Civil War. This was the experience of the young male of literary bent who was torn between a cultivated, gentle mother who fostered and encouraged that bent and a hard-bitten businessman father who wanted his eldest son to get out into the world and make money. The meaning of masculinity was central to this. I also found that for Page the conflict divided him not in two ways but three. A yearning to have political and social influence complicated the split between aesthetic leanings and moneymaking. Far from choosing one over the others, he spent his life trying to combine all three. Some of what I am describing later became the subject of Anne Douglas's *The Feminization of American Culture*. As soon as I read that book, I wrote her a fan letter that said, "Where were you when I needed you?"[11]

With Roosevelt and Wilson, this interest in them apart from preconceived concepts was even more exciting. I adopted an unusual but, for me, useful plan of attack for my research. Thanks to the uncanny parallels in their lives and the wealth of published and microfilmed sources on them, I plunged right into their papers for comparable chunks of their lives and afterward read secondary sources about those periods. I know this sounds like the dictum of the Queen of Hearts in *Alice in Wonderland*: "Sentence first! Verdict afterward." But this approach had precedent. Walter Prescott Webb once confessed that when he was working on *The Great Plains* he deliberately refrained from reading Frederick Jackson Turner because he wanted to come up with his own ideas, even if it meant repeating Turner. That was what I wanted to do too.[12]

What this approach allowed me to do was to modify and partly abandon the categorization of Roosevelt and Wilson as Nietzsche's warrior and priest. It is true that Theodore Roosevelt fitted the Nietzschean warrior as well as any statesman in history, but getting to know him on his own terms made me see him much better than relying too heavily on that categorization would have allowed. Roosevelt was capable of salutary restraint in the exercise of power. He was also capable of renouncing power, which spoke well for him but also had unfortunate results for his career.

It was with Wilson that this approach really failed. It did not take me long to discover that this man did not fit Nietzsche's priest model at all. He was not an idealist or ideologue who wanted power for the sake of making real the things in his mind. Rather, Wilson was just as much a believer in the primacy of power and affairs as was Roosevelt. In fact, I discovered that he was an anti-ideologue. The real significance of Wilson's attraction to Edmund Burke was not that it made him a conservative in current affairs. It was that he grasped the living, organic nature of human affairs and the perniciousness of trying to make people fit and submit to the prescriptions of ideologies. I still remember the afternoon that I was reading one of Wilson's Burkean essays when I said to myself, "This is *The End of Ideology*." By that, I meant the title of Daniel Bell's 1960 book and his and other liberals' eschewal of grand intellectual designs at that time.[13]

Avoiding your predecessors' writings has its risks and drawbacks. The risk is what Webb recognized when he avoided Turner: He might be repeating what had gone before him. There is, therefore, an inescapable obligation to read your predecessors carefully in order to discover where you are original and where you are not. In the case of Roosevelt, I found that I was following in the footsteps of George Mowry and John Morton Blum. When I read their works, I was continually struck by how right they had gotten it with Roosevelt. What I was doing, I hoped, was traveling further down the trail that they had begun to blaze.[14]

With Wilson, however, I found myself largely on my own. Of my predecessors, I found that only Arthur Link had begun to see Wilson the way I did, and Link had done that only in the later volumes of his Wilson biography. In those volumes, he had quietly overturned his central interpretation of Wilson in the earlier volumes and in his widely read book, Woodrow Wilson and the Progressive Era. I was doing more openly what Link had done quietly. I was rejecting the Nietzschean priest view of Wilson as an uptight, rigid, self-righteous, sometimes messianic idealist who could not bend to the needs of the real world. I also overturned the view that Link, Richard Hofstadter, and many others had propounded of Wilson as a conservative who became a progressive slowly, reluctantly, and strictly opportunistically. Instead, I recognized that Wilson was always a worldly thinker, a person who loved power almost as much as Roosevelt did, and someone whose political evolution had really gone from disengagement to engagement and from the general to the particular.[15]

Those are perhaps the most important advantages that I gained from picking subjects who interested me in and of themselves, apart from any views and ideas that I brought to them. Frankly, I distrust any biographer who does not have a similar interest. This is what allows her or him to question and change preconceived ideas and to appreciate the subject in a richer and truer way.

Now let me turn to my second "c" topic—conversation. In one way, all biographies are conversations with their subjects. By reading their written words or, with many subjects since the 1930s, listening to their recorded voices or watching their actions on film or videotape, biographers engage in conversations with their subjects. Most of those conversations—but not all—consist of listening to the subjects, then questioning and talking back to them by examining their actions, motives, and thoughts. That conversation can sometimes take bizarre forms. I have never had a dream in which I talked to one of my subjects, but I have seen and heard them in dreams. Once, in the case of Page, I awoke in a cold sweat, worried about whether I was being fair to him and maybe wrongfully imposing my view of him. Such experiences do count as conversations.

What interests me most, however, about biographers' conversations is something less common: when biographers can actually talk to and mine the memories of their subjects and people who knew them. In some cases, the subject is still living and the biographer can talk directly to her or him. Two of my favorite recent examples are Randall Woods's biography of William Fulbright and Robert Goldberg's biography of Barry Goldwater.[16] Both of them have told me that they gained a lot from meeting and talking with their subjects, but they have also told me that what they gained was a feeling for those men rather than specific information. They have said that friends, family, and associates were more helpful for specifics and perspectives.

My subjects were long dead by the time I came to study them. In fact, they had been gone so long that I had few opportunities to talk with anyone who had known them. Personal encounters came in my work on Page. An aged nephew of his gave me some valuable personal impressions, as did the economic historian Broadus Mitchell, who, when a boy, had met Page. Most of my conversations with people who knew my subjects have been secondhand, that is, reminiscences about them, and others' interviews of their contemporaries. This is called "oral history." That term has long amused me. It is a fancy name for something that people have been doing since time immemorial. Even the ancients talked to their subjects when they could, and picked the brains of their friends and foes.

In its twentieth-century usage, "oral history," the systematic search for and recording of memories of a subject, antedates the coining of the term. It really began with the biographers of two of my subjects. Both Page's and Wilson's first, authorized biographers were journalists—Burton J. Hendrick and Ray Stannard Baker. This pair did what came naturally to them. They interviewed people who had known their subjects. They sought out reminiscences. They targeted their inquiries to shed light on particular aspects of their subjects' lives and events in their careers. Finally, they preserved transcripts of their interviews and copies of the letters they received for use by others. They were practicing oral history two decades before the term was coined because they were doing things that it had never occurred to them not to do.[17]

Hendrick's and Baker's records of their interviews and the reminiscing correspondence that they solicited constitute vital records about their subjects, second in importance only to the actual correspondence and diaries by and about the men. In addition, Baker had Wilson's brother-in-law, Stockton Axson, read and criticize the manuscript of the biography. Axson's observations give a kind of blow-by-blow commentary on Wilson's life. At about the same time, in the 1920s, Axson also wrote a memoir of his acquaintance with Wilson, although it was not published until 1993. That book ranks alongside Owen Wister's *Roosevelt: The Story of a Friendship* as the most intimate and insightful account of its subject by a contemporary. Comparing what Axson wrote in that memoir with his comments on Baker's manuscript adds to the insights about Wilson.[18]

With the Wilson oral histories there is an additional advantage. In the late 1930s Henry W. Bragdon reinterviewed many of the people whom Baker had talked to a decade earlier. Bragdon was also able to talk to some people who had either refused to talk to Baker or had spoken with him only guardedly. This second round of interviews provides both more information and a second set of perspectives on Wilson's earlier years. Another of Wilson's journalist-biographers, William Allen White, interviewed a number of people, including some of Wilson's enemies. Unfortunately, White does not seem to have saved his notes from those interviews. If he had, it would be possible to use those notes along with the work done by Baker and Bragdon to triangulate Wilson in people's memories.[19]

That kind of triangulation or multiple perspective is even more important in oral history than in traditional document-based work. There is an old Chinese saying, "Palest ink is stronger than brightest memory." Fresh ink isn't always completely reliable, however. The clearest examples of this come from diaries. My first subject, Page, kept sporadic diaries, and it is sometimes possible to compare what he says there with what it says in other contemporary documents. Page was pretty reliable, but the way things looked to him did not always square with how they looked to others.

With Wilson, the problem is more acute. The greatest diary about him was kept by his close friend and adviser, Edward M. House. Everyone who works on Wilson and his politics and foreign policy between 1913 and 1920 has to rely on Colonel House's diary. This indispensable source provides information about Wilson's thought and actions that often cannot be found anywhere else. But the great problem with House's diary is that it stands alone for most of the time that he knew Wilson.[20]

As others have noted, people who keep diaries and write memoirs rarely portray themselves in a bad light, and they almost never minimize their own importance. This is especially so with Colonel House. Furthermore, he was a devious, manipulative person. His diary has to be used with great caution, not so much because he tells lies—although he sometimes does—but more because he makes himself look more important, and Wilson less important, than he was. House also attributes motives and attitudes to Wilson that are questionable, especially in cases in which Wilson was not following House's advice as much as the colonel wanted him to.

Fortunately, there are two possible ways of checking on the reliability of the House diary. One way is to consult one of the few recorded comments that Wilson made about House to a third party. In August 1915, Wilson was in hot pursuit of Edith Bolling Galt and wrote intimate letters to her. The widow Galt had taken an instant dislike to House and may have been jealous of his intimacy with her suitor. Though he defended House to her, Wilson did admit that "you are right in thinking that intellectually he is not a great man. His mind is not of the first class. He is a counselor, not a statesman. And he has the faults of his qualities." That comment alone casts House in a different light from his self-portrait in his diaries.[21]

The other check on those diaries comes from 1919, when House and Wilson were at the peace conference in Paris. At the president's side were several other people who kept diaries. Particularly notable were Wilson's physician, Admiral Cary T. Grayson, and the chief press officer of the delegation and future Wilson biographer, Ray Stannard Baker. Frequently, Wilson would tell one of them, most often Grayson, about the same incidents and discussions that House described in his diary. Therefore, it is possible to have one or sometimes two sets of testimony to place alongside the House diary. What those checks show is chiefly that Wilson often had thoughts and motives other than the ones that the colonel attributed to him. For those months it really is possible to have a conversation among as well as with the sources.[22]

Thus far, I have not been talking about anything unusual among biographers. I have simply been recounting experiences that all biographers have. All of us have ways of choosing our subjects, and all of us have conversations with our subjects, one way or another. Let me turn now to something that is unusual, though not unique, among biographers: comparison.

Let me make something clear at the outset of this discussion on comparison. In one way, I am still treading the same ground that I have already trod. I am describing something that all biographers do. Every biographer makes comparisons between her or his subject and other people. Comparison is to biographers what the question of "what if?"—or, more pretentiously put, "counterfactualism"—is to historians. It is something that they cannot help doing, whether they admit it or not. Also, to keep the record straight, non-biographer historians do plenty of comparing, while biographers do plenty of asking "what if?" My favorite example of that comes from Mark Schorer's biography of Sinclair Lewis, in which he asks what Lewis's later life and literary career might have been like if he had gone to college somewhere besides Yale.[23]

The unusual element in my experience with comparison is the scale on which I undertook it. My book on Roosevelt and Wilson is not just a comparative study of the two men. That would be a fine thing to do. Plenty of historians and other writers have implicitly and explicitly compared their personalities, ideas, policies, actions, and accomplishments. Those kinds of comparisons originated, in fact, with the men themselves and their contemporaries. Such comparisons have tended to create the almost Kantian categories that have separated Rooseveltians from Wilsonians for generations since.

I once ducked a question about which man I liked more by repeating what a Texan supposedly said about his preferences in music: "There are two kinds of music—country and western—and I like them both." I spoke sincerely because there is a lot I do like in both men, and there is also plenty that I dislike in both of them. But I was ducking the question because the world really is divided into two sects, each worshipping one and despising the other. I tried my best to avoid taking sides, but in the eyes of some people I did not succeed.

The book I wrote is not a comparative study of these men. Rather, it is a comparative biography. I followed them in parallel through their lives. I told each man's story with an eye on the other. At first they led widely separated lives that truly did run parallel. But at a critical point in both of their lives, the parallel lines bent into intertwining ones and never again separated.

I do not pretend to be a unique practitioner of this form of biography. Coincidentally, my book appeared at roughly the same time as two other comparative biographies. One was Alan Brinkley's book on Huey Long and his fellow radical demagogue, Father Charles Coughlin. The other was John Thomas's biography of Edward Bellamy, Henry George, and Henry Demarest Lloyd. They did the same thing that I did. They examined and recounted their subjects' lives and careers in parallel and in conjunction, always with an eye on the other or others. More recently, Charles Royster has done a comparative biography of those two overweening Civil War generals, Stonewall Jackson and William Tecumseh Sherman. [24]

I think all these books succeeded in exploring dimensions of their subjects that could not be captured, or at least not captured so well, in single-life, freestanding biographies. If I may be immodest, I think I did fairly well at this job too.

Let me give some examples of what I believe I contributed by writing a comparative biography of Roosevelt and Wilson. Comparison is a matter of judging both similarities and differences. The similarities between these two men too often got lost, even in comparative studies of them. Nietzsche's warrior and priest seemed to explain them to most of the people who studied them, even when those students were not aware that they were using those categories. For me, there was a real danger that I might have remained enthralled by those categories if I had not ventured beyond a comparative study into a comparative biography.

Examining both men's early lives and first attractions to politics made the profound similarity, often identity, of their views unmistakable. I have already recounted how I came to reject the Nietzschean priest category for Wilson. Let me give another example of their profound similarity. One of the biggest surprises for anyone who looks at Wilson between 1898 and 1900 is discovering what an enthusiastic imperialist he was. Only a keen ear for the differences in the two men's styles enables one to tell Roosevelt's utterances about the Spanish-American War and its imperialist consequences from Wilson's. They were making the same two basic points. First, they argued that the acquisition of an overseas empire signified America's ascent into the ranks of the world's great powers—a development that they both welcomed. Second, they saw this event as a good thing in itself—and perhaps more important to them—they believed that this newfound involvement in world politics would supply a new, nobler, more elevating agenda for politics at home.

Let me dwell on this particular similarity just a bit longer. This was not just a case of Wilson's being an armchair Rooseveltian, somebody who cheered the troops and the fleet from the sidelines. According to Stockton Axson, Wilson was going through what was perhaps a mild midlife crisis at this time and told him, "I get so tired of a talking profession." There is no evidence that the forty-one-year-old Wilson thought of joining up and going to war, but it may well have crossed his mind. His deep discontent with the content of current politics led to an abortive collaboration with Roosevelt, whom he had met several years earlier. During his brief service as vice-president, Roosevelt hatched a plan to interest young men from Harvard, Yale, and Princeton in public affairs, and he invited Wilson to visit him at Sagamore Hill to discuss the idea in the summer of 1901. Roosevelt's sudden succession to the presidency soon afterward sidetracked that scheme, but when Wilson became president of Princeton the next year, Roosevelt applauded and exclaimed, "Woodrow Wilson is a perfect trump."[25]

This particular similarity also serves to illustrate the other advantage of comparative biography—exposing and delving into differences between the subjects. Unlike Wilson, Roosevelt did go off to fight, and he became a war hero and a rapidly rising political star. Why is there this difference?

I think it comes down to one thing—the disparity in their economic and social backgrounds and circumstances. Both men had young children, but Roosevelt was moderately wealthy and did not have to support his family through his earnings, as Wilson did.

F. Scott Fitzgerald said, "The rich are different from you and me." Ernest Hemingway retorted, "Yes, they have more money." But there is more to the difference than the comparative weights of Wilson's and Roosevelt's pocketbooks. I would amplify Fitzgerald's comment to note that it makes a huge difference by what means and how long ago the rich people in question acquired their money and the social standing that went with it.

The most striking difference between Roosevelt's and Wilson's backgrounds—even more striking than their families' being on opposite sides in the Civil War—was that Roosevelt belonged to an aristocracy. He came from a family that had enjoyed wealth and social position for so long that it could and did disdain newcomers to the ranks of the wealthy, and the moneygrubbing practices that had gotten them there. An individual's pursuits were to be valued more than his wealth. Such pursuits might include art, science, literature, learning, public service, and, in Roosevelt's view, military service. Roosevelt defied his social peers' disdain for politics by becoming a quasi-professional politician, but aristocratic assumptions and values always guided him, even when he believed he was most radical in his policies and programs. Much about Roosevelt really did come down to an effort to preserve aristocratic values in a democratic and materialistic time and place.

Contrast Roosevelt and Wilson. As a youth, Wilson was equally attracted to politics and public service. He would have loved to take the route that Roosevelt took. But he had neither the wealth nor the social status of the other man. I am not trying to make Wilson seem a commoner. He came from a social and intellectual elite within his region and culture—the ministry, specifically, the Presbyterian ministry. But such a background made him what is now called a "meritocrat"—an exemplar and exponent of the triumph of talent, particularly intellectual talent. Moreover, unlike Roosevelt, he did not come from the richest and most powerful part of the country. Rather, he hailed from an impoverished and defeated hinterland. Of course Wilson had advantages, but those paled in comparison with those that Roosevelt's position afforded him. Wilson coined the term "man on the make," and much of his educational and political career did come down to an effort to promote the continuing rise of those with talent who came from below and outside the dominant circles of wealth and power.

One advantage that I derived from appreciating this profound difference in social background and conditioning between Roosevelt and Wilson was the ability to grasp how truly great an intellectual and ideological divide separated them and their political visions when they ran against each other in the 1912 election — Roosevelt's New Nationalism and Wilson's New Freedom. The dominant view of their campaigns was, and for many probably still is, summed up in William Allen White's celebrated quip: "Between the New Nationalism and the New Freedom was that fantastic imaginary gulf that has always existed between tweedle-dum and tweedle-dee." It is easy to support that view by noting how similar their stands were on specific issues and how little either man was able to appeal beyond traditional party followings. That view also meshes nicely with Roosevelt's charges that Wilson was an insincere, Johnny-come-lately progressive — the view that Arthur Link espoused in his earlier works on Wilson. [26]

I think that view is totally wrong. I think that the differences in the ideas expressed under the rubrics of the New Nationalism and the New Freedom were so deep and interesting that the de facto debate between their exponents verged on political philosophy. They differed fundamentally in their prescriptions for achieving the good society and in their conceptions of human nature that underlay those prescriptions. For all his sincerely professed "radicalism," Roosevelt embodied a classic conservative's dim view of human nature, which required that people somehow rise above themselves and their self-interests — in this instance, to be evangelized by the transcendent vision of the "New Nationalism." For all his Calvinist background, Wilson embodied a classic liberal's bright view of human nature, which exhorted people to be themselves and pursue their self-interests — in this instance, to be energized by efforts to reopen unfairly closed channels of opportunity and thereby attain a "New Freedom." I have said it before, and I will say it again: I think this was the greatest campaign in American history—bar none. Of course, doing a comparative biography was not the only way to come to an appreciation of the profundity of their differences, but it certainly helped. Knowing what brought the two men to where they stood in that campaign serves better than anything else to make one recognize what was at stake.

Finally, on this point, let me turn away from my own experience to make a comment on this type of biography. There are some other comparative biographies around. I have named four that have appeared in the last twenty years. Comparison is a rich and fascinating approach. But I also think it is a severely limited approach. I believe that comparative biography has limited application because there are relatively few historical figures who are truly comparable. In order for this approach to work for the historian-biographer, the subjects need to be at least roughly contemporary and to have interacted with each other. It can be argued that in other fields, such as literature or science, it would be possible to do comparative biographies of people who were widely separated in time or unknown to each other. I think, however, that subjects such as these push the work back into comparative study. For comparative biography in other fields, I think you need subjects to have been contemporaries and at least known of each other. Bach and Handel might be good candidates for a comparative biography, if one does not already exist.

Comparative biography is a powerful method. From my own experience I believe that this approach can supply perspectives that yield rich results that may not be attainable otherwise. But that experience also led me to believe that this approach is extremely limited. There are lots of subjects who can lend themselves to dual biographies with some comparative features. Three examples that come to mind are Abraham Lincoln and Stephen Douglas, Dwight D. Eisenhower and Douglas MacArthur, and John F. Kennedy and Richard M. Nixon.[27] But I do not think that in the end truly comparative biographies of these subjects can be written. I wish this method had a wider applicability, but I do not think it has. For myself, despite my delight and respect for this approach, I have no plans to write another comparative biography. My most recent work, a study of the debate and conflict over American membership in the League of Nations—better known as the "League fight"—featured Wilson as the leading actor and further fired my fascination with him. As a result, I am about to embark on a one-volume biography of him.[28]

For now, those three c's—conception, conversation, and comparison—encompass nearly all of what I would like to pass on from my experience as a biographer. I have no grand synthesis to offer. Nor do I have a grand vision for the bold new ventures in biography. These lacks may indicate only a failure of imagination on my part. But, at the risk of immodesty, let me assert that there is something else behind my limitations. I think it is the nature of biography itself. As I observed at the beginning of this chapter, the only way anyone really learns to be a biographer is by doing it: There is no substitute for experience.

Notes

1. Those were "William E. Borah, Political Thespian," *Pacific Northwest Quarterly* 56 (October 1965): 145–53, and *The Vanity of Power. American Isolationism and the First World War, 1914–1917* (Westport CT: Greenwood Press, 1969).

2. *Walter Hines Page: The Southerner as American, 1855–1918* (Chapel Hill: University of North Carolina Press, 1977).

3. *The Warrior and the Priest: Woodrow Wilson and Theodore Roosevelt* (Cambridge: Harvard University Press, 1983).

4. Catherine Drinker Bowen discusses this matter in *The Writing of Biography* (Boston: The Writing, 1951) and *Adventures of a Biographer* (Boston: Little, Brown, 1959). The other books of hers to which I referred are *John Adams and the American Revolution* (Boston: Little, Brown, 1950) and *Family Portrait* (Boston: Little, Brown, 1970).

5. Stanley Coben, *A. Mitchell Palmer, Politician* (New York: Columbia University Press, 1963).

6. William Holmes, *The White Chief: James Kimble Vardaman* (Baton Rouge: Louisiana State University Press, 1970).

7. David Levy, *Herbert Croly of the New Republic* (Princeton NJ: Princeton University Press, 1985).

8. T. Harry Williams, *Huey Long* (New York: Alfred A. Knopf, 1969).

9. Burton J. Hendrick, *The Training of an American* (Boston: Little, Brown, 1928).

10. Robert Osgood, *Ideals and Self-Interest in America's Foreign Relations: The Great*

Twentieth Century Transformation (Chicago: University of Chicago Press, 1953), 144–45.

11. Ann Douglas, *The Feminization of American Culture* (New York: Alfred A. Knopf, 1977).

12. Walter Prescott Webb, "History as High Adventure," in *An Honest Preface and Other Essays* (Boston: Houghton Mifflin, 1959), 214.

13. Daniel Bell, *The End of Ideology* (New York: Collier, 1960).

14. John Morton Blum, *The Republican Roosevelt* (Cambridge: Harvard University Press, 1954); George Mowry, *Theodore Roosevelt and the Progressive Movement* (Madison: University of Wisconsin Press, 1946).

15. Arthur S. Link, *Wilson*, 5 vols. (Princeton NJ: Princeton University Press, 1947–1965); Link, *Woodrow Wilson and the Progressive Era, 1910–1917* (New York: Harper, 1954).

16. Robert Goldberg, *Barry Goldwater* (New Haven CT: Yale University Press, 1995) and Randall Woods, *Fulbright: A Biography* (New York: Cambridge University Press, 1995).

17. Burton J. Hendrick, *The Life and Letters of Walter Hines Page*, 3 vols. (Garden City NY: Doubleday, Page, 1922–1925), and Ray Stannard Baker, *Woodrow Wilson: Life and Letters*, 8 vols. (Garden City NY: Doubleday, Page, 1927–1939).

18. Stockton Axson, *"Brother Woodrow": A Memoir of Woodrow Wilson* (Princeton NJ: Princeton University Press, 1993), and Owen Wister, *Roosevelt: The Story of a Friendship* (New York: Macmillan, 1930).

19. Henry W. Bragdon, *Woodrow Wilson: The Academic Years* (Cambridge: Harvard University Press, 1967), and William Allen White, *Woodrow Wilson: The Man, His Times, and His Task* (Boston: Houghton Mifflin, 1924).

20. The House Diary is in the Yale University Library. Much of it was published, under House's sponsorship, in a sometimes-bowdlerized version as Charles Seymour, ed., *The Intimate Papers of Colonel House*, 4 vols. (Boston: Houghton Mifflin, 1926–1928).

21. Wilson to Edith Bolling Galt, 28 August 1915, *The Papers of Woodrow Wilson*, ed. Arthur S. Link, 34 (Princeton NJ: Princeton University Press, 1980), 352.

22. *Papers of Woodrow Wilson*, ed. Link, vols. 53–61.

23. See Mark Schorer, *Sinclair Lewis: An American Life* (New York: McGraw-Hill, 1961).

24. Alan Brinkley, *Voices of Protest: Huey Long, Father Coughlin and the Great Depression* (New York: Alfred A. Knopf, 1983); John L. Thomas, *Alternative America: Edward Bellamy, Henry George, Henry Demarest Lloyd, and the Adversary Tradition* (Cambridge:

Harvard University Press, 1983), and Charles Royster, *Destructive War: William Tecumseh Sherman, Stonewall Jackson, and the Americans* (New York: Alfred A. Knopf, 1991).

25. Ray Stannard Baker interview with Stockton Axson, 12 March 1925, Ray Stannard Baker Papers, Library of Congress, box 99; Roosevelt to Cleveland H. Dodge, 16 June 1902, *The Letters of Theodore Roosevelt*, ed. Elting E. Morison (Cambridge: Harvard University Press, 1951), 3:275.

26. White, *Wilson*, 264.

27. I am indebted to Professor Kenneth Winkle of the University of Nebraska–Lincoln for suggesting Lincoln and Douglas as subjects for comparative biography.

28. The book on the League fight is *Breaking the Heart of the World: Woodrow Wilson and the Fight for the League of Nations* (New York: Cambridge University Press, 2001).

Selected Bibliography

Bowen, Catherine Drinker. *Adventures of a Biographer*. Boston: Little, Brown, 1959.

———. *Family Portrait*. Boston: Little, Brown, 1964.

———. *The Writing of Biography*. Boston: The Writer, 1951.

Brinkley, Alan. *Voices of Protest: Huey Long, Father Coughlin and the Great Depression.* New York: Alfred A. Knopf, 1983.

Coben, Stanley. *A. Mitchell Palmer: Politician*. New York: Columbia University Press, 1963.

Cooper, John Milton, Jr. *Walter Hines Page: The Southerner as American*. Chapel Hill: University of North Carolina Press, 1977.

———. *The Warrior and the Priest: Woodrow Wilson and Theodore Roosevelt.* Cambridge: Harvard University Press, 1983.

Douglas, Ann. *The Feminization of American Culture*. New York: Alfred A. Knopf, 1977.

Goldberg, Robert Alan. *Barry Goldwater*. New Haven: Yale University Press, 1995.

Royster, Charles. *Destructive War: William Tecumseh Sherman, Stonewall Jackson and the Americans*. New York: Alfred A. Knopf, 1997.

Thomas, John L. *Alternative America: Edward Bellamy, Henry George, Henry Demarest Lloyd, and the Adversary Tradition*. Cambridge: Harvard University Press, 1983.

Williams, T. Harry. *Huey Long*. New York: Alfred A. Knopf, 1969.

Woods, Randall B. *Fulbright: A Biography*. New York: Cambridge University Press, 1995.

5. Ut *Pictura Poesis*; or, The Sisterhood of the Verbal and Visual Arts

Nell Irvin Painter

As a biographer, I propose to bring together two ordinarily separate fields, black studies and art history. I urge biographers—particularly of subaltern subjects—to break their methodological habits and make full use of pictures. "Subaltern subjects" refers to individuals who are oppressed on account of their group identity, for instance, white women and members of stigmatized minorities. In recognition of the possibility of subaltern subjects' exercising power over others, the term "subaltern" conveys the complexity of subordinate identities. Images contain a wealth of meaning about biographical subjects and about the cultural and historical conventions that mold subaltern identities.

African American studies understandably regards European cultural history with a certain distrust, for Western civilization has denigrated people of African descent since the institutionalization of the Atlantic slave trade and the building of American culture around the political economy of African slavery. Scholarship and popular culture express their negrophobia differently; whereas much scholarship pretends black people do not exist, popular culture has offered an abundance of stereotypes. Before the late twentieth century, black people all too often appeared in words or pictures as objects of insult. The combination of blindness and indignity still dismays Africana scholars and discourages us from burrowing too deeply into Western thought.

Wary though we may be of the negrophobia and stereotypes of Euro-centric thought, we use its tools and adopt its postures, unwittingly, and practically by default. Like our Eurocentric counterparts, we are attracted to images and subjected to their power at the same time that we neglect them as sources of knowledge. We are no more likely than our counter-parts to realize that our automatic downgrading of images comes from the Western intellectual history of which we are inadvertent heirs. If we can see, historicize, and resist this prejudice against images as sources of knowledge, we may draw on the pictorial as well as the written record of our subjects' lives.

We need to separate the insight from scholarship's bias against images and in favor of words. We need to recognize what can be learned from images in historical space. We need to rejoin images that scholarship segregates but that biographical subjects experienced. Scholars of liter-ature and art history have already recognized the influence of stereotype in subaltern self-fashioning and autobiography. Like critics, biographers can also use images to explore their subjects and their subjects' cultural milieux. Biographers, who enjoy enormous appeal among readers and publishers, need to exploit the relationship of writing and images.

My title comes from a phrase in the Ars Poetica of Horace (65–8 BCE) that literally means "as in painting, so in poetry" and is also translated as "the sisterhood of the arts." Despite its classical roots and wording, the phrase ut pictura poesis is most closely associated with two other historical eras: the Western European Renaissance and the post-1960s. Earlier, the sisterhood of the arts appeared in discussions of mimesis: imitations of nature. Today the sisterhood of the arts is far more likely to appear in semiotics: the analysis of signs whose meanings depend on the cultural contexts in which they appear.

In both the Renaissance and the post-1960s, ut pictura poesis refers to the sisterhood of the arts, a sisterhood that holds whether "arts" are defined narrowly—as painting and poetry—or broadly—as images and texts.[1] Ut pictura poesis differs from paragone, which pits poetica against pictura and argues for the supremacy of pictura as a means of reflecting nature.[2] Un-like paragone, ut pictura poesis stresses complementarity. Complementarity conveys the consensus of current analysts of the image, including W. J. T. Mitchell, Martine Joly, Ernst Gombrich, and Nelson Goodman.[3]

The critic W. J. T. Mitchell cited the ancient Greek poet Simonides of Ceos (c. 556–468 BCE) as the inventor of the ut pictura poesis tradition.[4] However, the theme of the relationship between pictures and words appeared in Plato and Aristotle as well as in Horace's Ars Poetica, from which the phrase comes. Simonides, Plato, Aristotle, and the Renaissance thinkers who used them drew parallels between painting and poetry based on one aim: They all assumed mimesis—the capture or imitation of nature—to be the role of both pictures and writing. Post-structuralism and semiotics revived ut pictura poesis in the 1960s, as art historians like W. J. T. Mitchell built upon the thought of French structuralists and post-structuralists such as Roland Barthes.[5] In the 1950s and 1960s, Barthes showed how images, seemingly natural representations of reality, are actually highly stylized symbols full of cultural meaning. Barthes coined the oft-repeated phrase "rhetoric of the image" in a 1964 essay of the same name in the journal Communications.[6]

Just as I join these art historians in stressing complementarity, I recognize with them other scholars' dependence on words and neglect of images as sources of meaning. For more than 250 years, scholars of all sorts have turned to written documents for source material. Biographers habitually mine texts, which they subject to careful analysis; however, they use visual source material uncritically, as mere illustration.

The neglect or thoughtless use of images cheats biographers and their audiences of the valuable information images contain. For an abundance of meaning emerges more clearly from images than from words. Biographers of even the most privileged subjects in the world tap new veins of meaning by reading images critically. In the case of subaltern biography, the neglect of images limits the field of biographers' critical thought. When the biographers' subjects have limited access to the written word, as is the case in much subaltern biography, the analysis of images becomes critical. Even when subjects are able to read, write, and convey written information to biographers, visual material reveals new dimensions in subjects' ambivalent relationship to their culture.

In this essay I consider themes of ut pictura poesis that both link and separate images and words. I then illustrate my discussion with three biographical examples: Frederick Douglass, Sojourner Truth, and Duke Ellington. This undertaking is interdisciplinary, as I draw from scholarship on biography, art history, and popular culture. Such an interdisciplinary approach captures the role of popular culture's stereotypes of black Americans, which the black feminist theorist Patricia Hill Collins called "controlling images."[7] For Collins, "controlling images" are negative stereotypes circulating in American popular culture about stigmatized groups. As powerful negative references, controlling images affect black behavior, and, by influencing behavior, controlling images transform biography. I apply her term to subaltern subjects generally, in this instance, to black men as well as women.

Using the phrase "controlling images" to convey the ideological dimension of black women's oppression, Collins evoked signs and their cultural meaning, i.e., semiotics.[8] She employed the word "images" metaphorically, for her "images" are mostly verbal. My use of her phrase is literal: I contrast visual controlling images with African Americans' visual self-fashioning to indicate two ways in which the analysis of images enriches biography: mimetically—by helping biographers more thoroughly portray nature—and semiotically—by helping them unpack the cultural meanings that images contain and convey. By relying on the sisterhood of the arts, biographers may gain more information, more truth, and a fuller understanding of conventions and their meaning.

In the early 1990s I belonged to the ranks of logocentric historian-biographers. Graduate school had trained me to pursue truth only as expressed in words. In subsequent years I mined new fields but still only through the medium of text and without questioning my attachment to words and my neglect of images. I only turned to the latter in the absence of the former. My biographical subject, Sojourner Truth, did not read or write. As a consequence, all relevant written source material is highly mediated. I learned much about Truth through her dictated writings and articles about her, but at a long remove, because her amanuenses and the authors of prose portraits of Truth used her as a device for scoring their own points, sometimes against each other.

Given the paucity and lack of reliability of written sources from Truth, ordinary historical documents served as indirect sources at best, as highly misleading fictions at worst. However, Truth did sit for photographic portraits, small *cartes-de-visite*, which she sold to support herself. I had to consider these portraits as a means of discovering how Truth presented herself. I had to learn to interpret—to read what Barthes called the "rhetoric of the image"—the photographic portraits she commissioned and distributed. My initial approach to Truth's images served the interests of mimesis. I wanted to discover more about the nature of Sojourner Truth. That is not where I ended.

Truth's photographs fed my early interest in this project: the interrogation of her cultural meanings, which exceed what she did during her lifetime. I stress the symbolic dimension of Truth's meaning because Truth, like many prominent African American figures, carries meanings tied to her race and gender, meanings that her behavior alone does not capture. Her significance as an American icon overshadows her life as an individual of a given historical period and specific accomplishments. Truth was a black woman in a racist, sexist culture; thus her persona acquired an added, semiotic dimension, which I address in my title, *Sojourner Truth, A Life, A Symbol*.[9]

The cover image of my biography of Truth (figure 1) characterizes her portraits, in which she never appears as enslaved, subservient, pitiable, comic, or exotic. Truth is alone in her photographs. Well and respectably clothed, she poses as an American bourgeoise, complete with book, knitting, glasses, and vase of flowers at her side. Conforming to conventions of celebrity portraiture, she looks a little past the camera in self-assured seriousness. Her posture is relaxed but upright, communicating an impression of easy composure. Truth's *cartes-de-visite* show a mature and intelligent bourgeoise who would not speak in dialect. With only the face and hands uncovered, hers is the opposite of a naked body.[10] Considered separate from contemporary depictions of black women—or the complete absence of depictions—this image appears totally unremarkable. But it did not exist outside such contexts.

Douglass and Truth sat for their portraits at a time when the triangle of invisibility, anthropological "types," and minstrelsy bounded the representation of black men and women. In 1850, the year Sojourner

Truth published her *Narrative of Sojourner Truth* and presented her life story to feminists and abolitionists, the Harvard naturalist Louis Agassiz commissioned a South Carolinian daguerreotypist to take "specimen" photographs of enslaved plantation workers (figure 2).

Agassiz's photos show black adults naked to the waist, facing the camera, captured as "types," such as became common throughout the colonized world for more than a century. The unnamed people who appear in these specimen photos are always foreign and nearly always of color. They do not represent themselves as individuals but as "types" of people, like exhibits in museums of natural history—precisely their instigators' intention. Today students of cultural studies see such photographs as prime examples of Othering, of establishing hierarchies of race and "civilization." This is not the way Sojourner Truth chose to present herself.

Truth also avoided the other typical representation of black women, the happy darky of minstrelsy and the cook-mammy of the illustrators of Harriet Beecher Stowe's best-selling 1851–52 novel, *Uncle Tom's Cabin.* Stowe's Aunt Chloe drew upon and phenomenally reinforced the stereotype of the dark-skinned, female plantation slave cook, invariably a fat, bossy mammy. Subsequent mammy figures are legion—the most famous comes from the twentieth-century descendant of *Uncle Tom's Cabin* in popular culture. Margaret Mitchell's 1936 novel *Gone with the Wind* and the 1939 movie it inspired brought Hattie McDaniel an Oscar for best supporting actress. (She was the first black actor to receive an Oscar, which remains a rare honor for black actors to this day.) This famous black woman of *Gone with the Wind* has no name beyond "Mammy." Her predecessors, too, existed only as satellites of white characters. By contrast, no other people appear in Sojourner Truth's photographs. She alone occupies the entire frame.

Minstrelsy, although predominantly a male medium, occasionally featured the odd blacked-up woman or men dressed as women. This undated image—literally a stereotype—circulated for some forty years in the late nineteenth and early twentieth centuries. Dressed in work clothes, this figure expresses unrestrained motion. Her dance takes her off her feet and thrusts her backward. Her big-lipped white mouth gapes open, her big feet and hands are spread wide apart. The very embodiment of

1. Cover, Nell Irvin Painter,
Sojourner Truth, A Life, A Symbol
(New York: W. W. Norton,
1996). The photo was taken in
1864 by an unidentified photographer. National Portrait
Gallery, Smithsonian Institution, Washington DC.

2. Daguerreotype by Louis
Agassiz. Joseph T. Zealy, 1850.
Courtesy of the Peabody Mu-
seum of Archaeology and Eth-
nology, Harvard University.
Photographs by Hillel Burger.

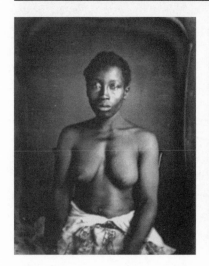

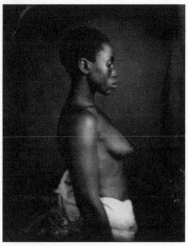

exuberance, she is the antithesis of respectability, dignity, poise (literally), and gravitas (literally). She manifests movement, not thought; silliness, not seriousness.

The female figure (figure 3) appears beside a male figure—also a clown—and cannot serve as the focal point in the image. Because he is upright and she practically falls down, her image is subordinate to his.

Sitting for her portraits afforded Sojourner Truth a means of documenting her presence as a citizen. Her portraits offer her biographers firsthand source material that her illiteracy otherwise denies. As rare images of a black woman, Truth's photographs testified to the fact of her existence.

Many more images exist of Truth's more famous, male colleague Frederick Douglass, which, in their abundance, convey additional meanings. The subject of numerous biographies and portraits in a variety of media, Douglass began to be painted and photographed in the mid-1840s, nearly twenty years before Truth first sat before a photographer. Whereas Truth's portraits appear in a vacuum, Douglass's images reflect his self-fashioning and his supporters' notions of appropriate schema.

An abundance of words and images makes Frederick Douglass (1817–1895)—fugitive slave, abolitionist, and America's leading nineteenth-century black statesman—an ideal example of the ways in which the use of visual material can buttress biography. Douglass is one of the few African American subjects of more than two full-length, adult biographies.[11] (W. E. B. Du Bois, Booker T. Washington, and Duke Ellington join Douglass in having multiple biographies.) Two generations' worth of thoughtful biographies based on written sources trace Douglass's trajectory, capture his words and ideas, and weigh his influence on American politics, but none scrutinizes his self-concept and persona as expressed through images. Thanks to the existence of *Majestic in His Wrath: A Pictorial Life of Frederick Douglass*, a 1995 exhibition and catalogue from the Smithsonian American Portrait Gallery, a biographical exploration of Douglass through portraiture is now possible.[12] By adding valuable information to what we already know about him, Douglass's portraits contribute to the work of mimesis.

Douglass escaped from slavery in Maryland in 1838 with the help of his fiancée Anna Murry, whom he married in New York City before moving

3. Minstrel Couple.

to New Bedford, Massachusetts. Douglass began speaking at antislavery meetings in the early 1840s, and by the mid-1840s he had become well known by dint of his persuasiveness as a speaker and the publication of the first of his three autobiographies, *Narrative of the Life of Frederick Douglass, an American Slave*, in 1845. Three portraits exist from the antebellum era: a painting, a daguerreotype, and an engraving.

According to the commentary in *Majestic in His Wrath*, this portrait (figure 4) represents "a visual testament to Douglass's enormous value to the antislavery cause. As an observer at one of Douglass's abolitionist appearances in 1842 put it, this 'fine specimen of an orator,' who invited favorable comparisons with no less than Daniel Webster, was 'a living, speaking, *startling* proof of the folly, absurdity and inconsistency . . . of slavery.' "[13]

In this portrait, Douglass's image largely conforms to the conventions of great portraiture. He appears alone, centered and filling the frame. The face turns slightly away from the viewer; the large, clear eyes look back at the viewer confidently, but with an air of preoccupation, probably with the great issue of the day, slavery. The hair waves but does not kink; the skin is colored, but not too dark.[14] A clean, white linen collar frames the handsome, pleasant face. Douglass's manly shoulders are extremely broad, but clothed in a beautifully tailored, fine black suit and brown waistcoat. The abstract background complements his skin color, and clothing strengthens the impression of transcendental beauty. The impression of refinement and subdued power corroborates the caption's quote from the "observer" who saw proof, in Douglass, "of [slavery's] folly, absurdity and inconsistency." Such a beautiful, sensitive image refuted the logic of slavery—but, perhaps, to the point of provoking disbelief.

A few years after the painting of the portrait above, Douglass sat for a daguerreotype (figure 5).

In this, Douglass fills the frame as completely as in his painted image, but the impression here is more of contained power than sensitive beauty. Douglass's color is darker; his eyes are not so large and open; his brow is more deeply furrowed, almost into a scowl; and his lips have not quite found the smile that hints of composed self-assurance. He still wears white linen with a cravat (this time light in color rather than dark, and

4. Frederick Douglass painting. Unidentified artist. Oil on canvas, 69.9 x 57.2 cm (27 1/2 x 22 1/2 in.), circa 1845. National Portrait Gallery, Smithsonian Institution, Washington DC.

5. Frederick Douglass daguerreotype. "Frederick Douglass in His Thirties," unidentified photographer, daguerreotype, 8.3 x 7 cm (3 1/4 x 2 3/4 in.), circa 1850–1855.

more completely framing a dark face), a black suit, and a waistcoat. But the shoulders are less wide and the clothing less perfectly tailored. Most striking to this viewer is the hair, here visibly African, despite careful combing. This Douglass, betraying hints of anger or distrust, is conceivable as a former slave, for his demeanor conveys less complacency and his complexion appears less smoothly flawless than in the painted portrait. This Douglass has known fear and rage.

A detour from this daguerreotype of Douglass leads to a daguerreotype portrait of Douglass's colleague on the antislavery circuit, Charles Lenox Remond (figure 6).

A few years older than Douglass, Remond (1810–1873) had been born free in Salem, Massachusetts. He and Douglass toured together in the 1840s. Although Douglass quickly began to outshine Remond as a public figure, they remained colleagues, not only against slavery, but also in favor of women's suffrage. Remond belongs to the legion of distinguished black Americans without full-length, scholarly biographies. When his appears, I hope it will follow Remond's visual clues of self-fashioning. Historiography invariably describes him merely as African American. But this daguerreotype presents an additional dimension of his identity, his Native American lineage and culture.

Today brown-skinned Massachusetts Indians appear regularly in courts of law to protect their tribal rights. In the 1850s Remond was telling everyone looking at his portrait that he was Indian as well as African. Frederick Douglass's daguerreotype contains no Indian iconography, such as Remond's hairdo. But regarded in light of Remond's hair, Douglass's facial features raise questions about his ethnic background that biographers have so far ignored.[15]

The 1845 engraved frontispiece of the Narrative of the Life of Frederick Douglass (figure 7) falls between the painted and daguerreotype portraits. Here Douglass appears less romantic than in the painting, less coiled than in the daguerreotype. The floppy cravat reinforces the literary appearance of the gentleman above the signature and corroborates the subtitle of his narrative: Written by Himself.

These three portraits of Frederick Douglass present a schema he controlled, in terms of the media (paint, photograph, engraving) and the

6. Charles Remond daguerreotype. Samuel Broadbent (1810–
1880). Daguerreotype, 10.8 x 8
cm (4 1/4 x 3 1/8 in.), circa 1850.
Boston Public Library/Rare
Books Department—Courtesy of
the Trustees.

7. Narrative frontispiece and title
page, Frederick S. Voss, *Majestic
in His Wrath: A Pictorial Life of
Frederick Douglass* (Washington
DC: National Portrait Gallery and
the National Park Service, United
States Department of the Interior
by the Smithsonian Institution
Press, 1995). Courtesy of the Library Company of Philadelphia,
Pennsylvania.

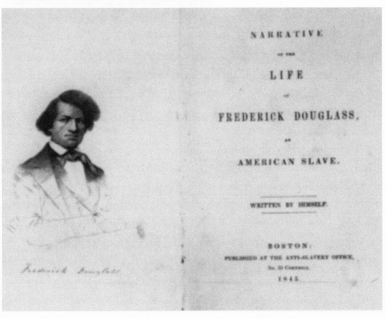

way he presented himself in dress and pose. None of these three portraits includes the kind of background that usually appears in the studio images of the 1860s. Nonetheless it is clear—from his posture and his dress—that Douglass is a man of the indoors. He looks more or less refined, more or less authentic, more or less literary in each representation. The differences among them shrink further in comparison with another contemporary image of Douglass, which appears on the cover of sheet music by the Hutchinson singers, the musical stalwarts of the antislavery movement. Douglass's self-fashioning effaces visual traces of his slave origins and emphasizes his mastery of the codes of gentlemanly autonomy. The Hutchinson music's image, however, connects him to his degraded past (figure 8).

In both its iconography and its caption, this image reinforces Douglass's connection to slavery. Barefooted and in work clothes (a loose, open-necked, patterned shirt, no tie, light-colored trousers), Douglass carries his meager belongings in a pillowcase and holds a cudgel. The slave catchers in the background to the left (barely visible in this reproduction, unfortunately) remind viewers that he is in peril and that he is owned. The trees and bushes put him out of doors and in proximity to nature. The words surrounding the image also reinforce Douglass's usefulness as an antislavery icon: "The Fugitive's Song," "A Graduate from the Peculiar Institution," "His Brothers in Bonds," "Fugitives from Slavery." This was emphatically not Douglass's own self-fashioning, not as a young man, not as an elder statesman.

Throughout his life Douglass continued to protest racial injustice, even though the success of his greatest cause propelled him out of the role of radical and into the rank of éminence grise. Times changed as well, so that the Great Man of the Gilded Age, the stalwart of the reigning Republican party dressed and expressed himself differently from the younger, antebellum abolitionist. Two post–Civil War portraits—one photographic, the other sculptural—materialize his mature greatness in conventional terms.

In about 1865 Douglass sat for Marcus Aurelius Root, the most skilled portrait photographer of the era and author of the 1864 photographic textbook The Camera and the Pencil, or, the Heliographic Art.[16] A master of the semiotics of every facet of photographic portrait making, Root set

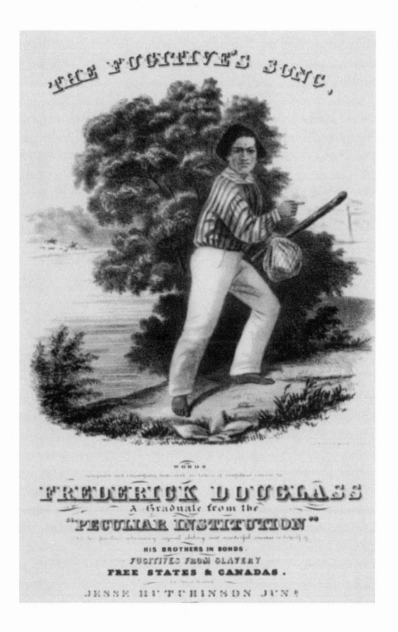

8. The Fugitive's Song. Courtesy of the Library Company of Philadelphia, Pennsylvania.

up his gallery with the intention of inspiring elevated thoughts in his esteemed sitters. Through the use of flattering lighting, focal lengths, poses, gazes, props, and clothing, Root aimed to reflect the greatness in each of his subjects. His portrait of Douglass (figure 9) combines gravitas with mellow beauty. Gone is the abundant white linen of the romantic era, replaced by an outfit almost clerical in its soberness. But Douglass now carries a gold-tipped cane, an emblem of royalty. The key light gently highlights the gray in his hair, now completely combed back from a regal forehead. Although Douglass no longer sports the part of his younger years, he still wears his hair long, a style suited to his moderately kinky (but not tightly coiled) hair. The professional polish of the photograph, combined with the elegance of Douglass, endow this image with colossal self-assurance.

The very fact of Root's having made his portrait confirms Douglass's elevation into elite ranks.[17] In Root's case, the artist's name bestows a certain standing upon the portrait. The Douglass bust (figure 10), by a less famous artist, expresses stateliness through the smooth, cool, and expensive medium of white marble. In the 1870s, when this bust was made, white marble, of itself, evoked Greco-Roman antiquity in all its civilized grandeur. The toga over Douglass's right shoulder alludes to imperial stature without obscuring the weight and drape of his splendid, late nineteenth-century clothing. This bearded Douglass combs his lightly waved hair back from a noble brow. Photographed by Root and captured in white marble, Douglass's postwar portraiture announced his accession into high public rank. None of his own portraits, whether before or after the Civil War and emancipation, linked him to slavery or hinted that his previous condition of servitude made him less a person, less a man, less a citizen of the Republic.

Writing *Sojourner Truth, A Life, A Symbol* in the 1990s and finding myself confronted with a problem of mimesis, I turned to her photographs as a means of completing her historical record. As I studied her images, however, I came to see that they testified in semiotic as well as mimetic terms; I could learn more about her, and I could make sense of her relation to her times. Both the visual conventions she avoided and those she adopted conveyed meaning. The schema of her culture omitted images of black

9. Frederick Douglass *carte-de-visite* by Samuel Root, circa 1865.

10. Frederick Douglass bust. Voss explains that Rochester, New York, citizens commissioned a marble portrait of Douglass by Johnson Mundy, a local sculptor, when he was leaving Rochester for Washington DC. Mundy completed the bust in 1873. The image reproduced here is actually a plaster replica made by C. Hess in about 1875. National Park Service, Frederick Douglass National Historic Site, Washington DC.

women. The few such images that existed were likely to be highly stereo-typed and/or degrading images of the black woman, not of a particular person, and certainly not having biographical intent.

Douglass's and Truth's portraits declare black Americans' continuing preoccupation with the documentation of their existence as people worthy of respect. Douglass's and Truth's imagery supplied information that, in its absence, was assumed not to exist. Douglass was cognizant of ne-grophobic stereotypes, but Duke Ellington's photographs from the 1920s and 1930s appeared in a popular culture full of degrading depictions and much closer in time to our own era. Ellington's image of elegant sophis-tication simultaneously contradicts and interrogates the racial caricature surrounding him—caricature that has faded from the historical record.

Absence was one fact of nineteenth-century black iconography; stereo-type was another. Frederick Douglass railed against the latter in 1849, well before the full elaboration of antiblack imagery of the following century: "Negroes can never have impartial portraits at the hands of white artists. It seems to us next to impossible for white men to take likenesses of black men, without most grossly exaggerating their distinctive features. And the reason is obvious. Artists, like all other white persons, have developed a theory dissecting the distinctive features of Negro physiognomy."[18]

In the nineteenth century (as in the twentieth and twenty-first), stereo-typical depictions of black people appeared far more frequently than those black people themselves projected. The increasing prevalence of all kinds of images in the twentieth century lent increased prominence to the antiblack, controlling images against which black self-fashioning contended. By the time Duke Ellington became well known, black bod-ies appeared often in American popular culture. Symbols of ridiculous fun, uproarious entertainment, or criminal menace, they remained ab-sent from depictions of respectability—except as servant-accoutrements. Duke Ellington, the subject of both conventional, text-based biography and abundant visual documentation, provides an ideal case study of the role of controlling images in black visual autobiography.

Edward Kennedy Ellington (1899–1974) was called "Duke" early on in tribute to his elegance. Ellington was born into a working-class fam-ily with ambitious style, and he credited his father, a butler, for having instilled in him the elegance that became his hallmark. Ellington is remembered as the composer of over one thousand pieces of music, large and small, including "Satin Doll," "Sophisticated Lady," "Don't Get around Much Anymore," "Do Nothing till You Hear from Me," and the longer "Black, Brown, and Beige." Today Ellington is recognized as a major American composer, but during his lifetime he performed indefatigably. Ellington became famous in the 1920s as the leader of the house band of the renowned Cotton Club of Harlem. Between 1927 and 1932 at the Cotton Club and through regular radio broadcasts, he laid the foundation of an eminence that has outlived him.

Ellington's image received national recognition in 1986, when he appeared on a U.S. postage stamp.[19] Here I depart from biographical tradition, which stresses Ellington's astonishingly original musical creativity, to concentrate on his iconography or, more expressly, on his elegance.[20] Two Ellington photographs (figure 11) from his 1933 tour of England express his characteristic polish. From the very beginning of his career, Ellington and his band dressed meticulously. He was famous for a bandbox appearance, which in his own case included carefully straightened ("conked") hair.

Both photos were taken from slightly below, so that much more of Ellington's body is visible than in ordinary portraits. The effect of pushing the head so far toward the top of the frame, putting the clothing in the middle, and effacing any background showcases Ellington's fashionable costume. The lighting in both photos sets off the texture of his clothing. With his hands in his trousers or jacket pockets, he appears jauntily at ease. The photo on the right (at least) has been retouched to outline the lapels of Ellington's long, double-breasted suit jacket. In both photos, Ellington wears just enough eye makeup to accentuate his personal glamour.

Virtually all of Ellington's photographs contain hallmarks of sophistication: conked hair; elegant, fashionable or formal clothing; a pose of relaxed self-assurance. Ellington smiles coolly, but his mouth never gapes open. He never grins or curries favor. He never tips his hat or cedes the image to white people. Polished and contained, he never, ever, wears blackface. In the 1920s the Ellington band lent sophistication to

11. Top: Two Ellington photographs, 1933.

12. Center left: The Famous Cotton Club. This image dates from 1930, when Cab Calloway's band had replaced Duke Ellington's. The photograph's caption makes no comment on the iconography of the Cotton Club program. Courtesy of James Gardiner.

13. Center Right: Duke Ellington Band.

14. Bottom: Minstrel Band.

the mystique of the Cotton Club of Harlem. Famous internationally, the Cotton Club (figure 12) advertised itself as a popular spot—"reservations advisable"—to a wealthy, sophisticated, nonblack clientele.

The doorman here wears the familiar big, red lips and ingratiating smile of American popular culture's black iconography. Smaller in size than the central white figures, he stands off to the side of the image and faces them. Although more of his face than theirs is visible, he attends to them, his arms spread apart in welcome. The incongruity of the broad stereotype of the black doorman's caricatured image and the relatively naturalistic depiction of the three white figures makes this a particularly unsettling image.

Ellington's own skin was a light medium brown, and most of his musicians' coloring ordinarily fell within the range from light to medium. While they did not all follow him into hair straightening, none of Ellington's musicians wore the obviously naturally kinky hair so prominent in stereotypes of black men. Even in work clothes, the Duke Ellington Band projected gentlemanly composure. In this photograph from 1935 (figure 13), Ellington and his band, all in formal attire, pose motionless with their instruments at their sides. They stand erect and handsome, wearing smiles, not grins. Everything speaks of self-control, of urbane manliness.

Compare the Ellington band's composure with this minstrel image (figure 14), which appears in books published in 1928 and 1936, when the Ellington band was playing at the Cotton Club. The minstrel band—composed of black men, not white men in blackface, to judge from the depiction of the lips and nappy hair—embodies the stereotypical blackness of controlling images. In a spirit of wild abandon, the musicians grin exuberantly. Knees spread wide, arms flung out from bodies, they are all in motion as they make what looks like cacophony. The central figure in the forefront of this band has his mouth wide open and his arms and legs spread wide. Everyone here wears outlandish clothing, as befits so bumbling a company. They are laughable, nay, downright ridiculous.

Self-fashioning such as Duke Ellington's occurred against a solid backdrop of controlling images on stage and screen mainly derived from minstrelsy. Although commonly identified with the crude white supremacy of the nineteenth century, minstrelsy flourished in American popular culture through the first half of the twentieth century. USO entertainment during World War II included blackface minstrelsy. "Amos 'n' Andy" lasted nearly forty years—and more than ten thousand broadcasts—on radio and television.[21]

Minstrelsy so dominated modernist New York theater that even the great breakthrough black shows and performers of the 1920s could not escape its reach. In Eubie Blake and Noble Sissle's 1921 Broadway hit Shuffle Along, the most influential black comedy team of the era, Flournoy Miller and Aubrey Lyles, appeared in blackface (figure 15). Even leading performers in this Harlem Renaissance showcase of black talent by black writers had to repeat the minstrel-darky tropes of open mouths, rolling eyes, white lips, and utter mystification.

Josephine Baker came out of the same milieu (figure 16). She began her rise to stardom in the New York entertainment world of Blake, Sissle, and Ellington, figuring in the chorus line of Shuffle Along and appearing in Sissle and Blake's second Broadway show, The Chocolate Dandies, in 1924. The crossed eyes and little-girl outfit could be seen on other contemporary female performers like Fannie Brice, but the white lips, spread legs, and gigantic feet come straight from minstrelsy and reproduce its Sambo-esque motifs.

Biographies of Ellington and histories of American popular culture seldom mention the plethora of stereotypical images that filled the entertainment media of his time. The silence from the black side of a long-standing color bar relates to the preservation of dignity: Not wishing to diminish their own humanity, black people refrained from commenting on these all-too-familiar but degrading images. In an article on Duke Ellington, the critic and essayist Albert Murray complained of this kind of self-censorship. Murray grumbled that black biographies and autobiographies read like "case histories" and "sociopolitical abstractions" intended to illustrate theories of blackness rather than evocations of real, fully rounded lives.[22]

Coming to terms with stereotype has been no easier on the other side of the color line. Nonblack observers and scholars also find minstrel images embarrassing and generally forego mention of everyday manifestations of the humiliation of Negroes. Unless an author's subject is antiblack

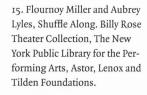

15. Flournoy Miller and Aubrey Lyles, Shuffle Along. Billy Rose Theater Collection, The New York Public Library for the Performing Arts, Astor, Lenox and Tilden Foundations.

16. Josephine Baker, 1924. Billy Rose Theater Collection, The New York Public Library for the Performing Arts, Astor, Lenox, and Tilden Foundations.

stereotype, the presence of these images ordinarily goes unremarked.[23]

Students of black identity, usually critics of literature and art rather than biographers, often note the role of stereotype in black people's self-fashioning. Herman Gray, for instance, notes that "self-representations of black masculinity in the United States are historically structured by and against dominant (and dominating) discourses of masculinity and race."[24] Scholars like Gray discuss cultural phenomena persuasively. But without biography's concentration on one life at a time and its revelation of the meaning of culture in a life examined at length, critics' work lacks the vividness we expect of biography. Readers turn to biography for the embodiment of abstraction, and biographers can apply critics' readings of cultural meaning at the level of individual life. By analyzing images as well as text, subaltern biographers can better bring their subjects to life within those subjects' cultural contexts.

Ut pictura poesis, the sisterhood of the arts, alerts biographers to the differences of medium that struck Gotthold Ephraim Lessing in the mid-eighteenth century and reminds them to exploit images' occupation of space. Subaltern biographers can come closer to nature—to truth—by reading the rhetoric of portraits. Attending to the dialectic of conventional and biographical imagery, subaltern biographers also enter the symbolic webs of meaning within which their subjects lived and fashioned themselves. Words tell only part of the story; the schema emerges from images as well. Ut pictura poesis reminds biographers to scrutinize images as well as texts and realize the full promise of the sisterhood of the arts.

Notes

1. Strictly speaking, any discussion of the sister arts ought to include music. But I limit myself here to the terms of the centuries-old tradition of ut pictura poesis: pictures and words.

2. During the Italian Renaissance, Leonardo da Vinci advanced paragone's most eloquent arguments. Today the historian of images Barbara Maria Stafford makes such a case emphatically, but not, to my mind, entirely convincingly. See Barbara Maria Stafford, Good Looking: Essays on the Virtue of Images (Cambridge: MIT Press, 1996), 4–8.

3. See Martine Joly, *Introduction à l'analyse de l'image* (Paris: Editions Nathan, 1993), 101–6. See also W. J. T. Mitchell, *Iconology: Image, Text, Ideology* (Chicago: University of Chicago Press, 1986), 8, 43–48, 61–77, 80–81, and Mitchell, "Ut Pictura Theorea," in *Picture Theory*, ed. W. J. T. Mitchell (Chicago: University of Chicago Press, 1994), 209–39.

4. W. J. T. Mitchell, "Spatial Form in Literature: Toward a General Theory," *The Language of Images*, ed. W. J. T. Mitchell (Chicago: University of Chicago Press, 1980), 289, and Mitchell, *Iconology*, 48, 116. In 520 BCE Simonides delivered the earliest recorded encomium (Greek laudatory song) in honor of victors in the Olympic Games. See Encyclopædia Britannica Online: "Simonides of Ceos" *http://www.eb.com:180/bol/topic?eu=69622&sctn=1&pm=1* and "encomium" *http://www.eb.com:180/bol/topic?eu=137492&sctn=1&pm=1*.

5. My using "semiotics" and "post-structuralism" interchangeably relies on their common genealogy and their stress on the importance of culture's influence on individual behavior and thought. Just as there exist several currents within semiotics, there also exist different sorts of post-structuralism, according to the period under review, the thinkers in question, and the methodology in use. Many of the leading 1960s French structuralists, such as Michel Foucault and Roland Barthes, are also considered leading post-structuralists. What I wish to emphasize in contrasting semiotics and post-structuralism, on the one hand, and pursuing the past as it really was, on the other, is the formers' emphasis on meaning, as opposed to the latter's faith in the transparency of fact. On the role of semiotics in *ut pictura poesis*, see Wendy Steiner, *The Colors of Rhetoric* (Chicago: University of Chicago Press, 1982).

6. Roland Barthes, "The Rhetoric of the Image," in *Image/Music/Text*, trans. Stephen Heath (1964; reprint, New York: Hill & Wang, 1977), 32–35. See also Barthes's essays in *Mythologies* (Paris: Collection Pierres Vives, 1957), and *La chambre claire: Note sur la photographie* (Paris: Cahiers du Cinéma Gallimard Seuil, 1980). Although Barthes's work is crucial in the development of semiology, he did not discuss *ut pictura poesis* by name.

7. Patricia Hill Collins, *Black Feminist Thought: Knowledge, Consciousness, and the Politics of Empowerment*, 2nd ed. (1990; reprint, New York: Routledge, 2000), 5, 69–88. See also Deborah Willis, ed., *Picturing US: African-American Identity in Photography* (New York: New Press, 1994), xi–xii, 3–26, and bell hooks, *Black Looks: Race and Representation* (Boston: South End Press, 1992).

8. Semiotics (or semiology) refers to the study of signs, which one of the field's founders, the nineteenth-century American philosopher, Charles Sanders

Peirce, defined as "something which stands to somebody for something." The other founder, the Swiss linguist Ferdinand de Saussure, described language as a system of signs, within which he distinguished words from concepts. Saussure's work in linguistics laid the groundwork for structuralism and post-structuralism, both of which stress the importance of social structure, or culture, in patterning individual human behavior and constructing meaning.

9. Robert F. Reid-Pharr discusses the cultural dimensions of African American life and identity in *Conjugal Union: The Body, the House, and the Black American* (New York: Oxford University Press, 1999), 3–12, 129–31.

10. For a fuller discussion of Truth's portraits, see Nell Irvin Painter, *Sojourner Truth, A Life, A Symbol* (New York: W. W. Norton, 1996), 185–99.

11. Important biographies of Frederick Douglass include the following: Philip S. Foner, *Frederick Douglass, A Biography* (New York: Citadel Press, 1964); Benjamin Quarles, *Frederick Douglass* (Englewood Cliffs NJ: Prentice-Hall, 1968); Waldo E. Martin, *The Mind of Frederick Douglass* (Chapel Hill: University of North Carolina Press, 1984); William S. McFeely, *Frederick Douglass* (New York: W. W. Norton, 1990).

12. Frederick Voss, *Majestic in His Wrath: A Pictorial Life of Frederick Douglass* (Washington DC: Smithsonian Institution Press for the National Portrait Gallery and the National Park Service, 1995).

13. Voss, *Majestic in His Wrath*, 22. Emphasis in original.

14. On nineteenth-century depictions of black men, see Richard Powell, "Cinqué," *American Art* 11 (fall 1997): 48–73, and Richard Yarborough, "Race, Violence, and Manhood: The Masculine Ideal in Frederick Douglass's 'The Heroic Slave,'" in *Frederick Douglass: New Literary and Historical Essays*, ed. Eric J. Sundquist (Cambridge: Cambridge University Press, 1990), 166–88.

15. The Douglass daguerreotype also contains hints that Douglass might have shared an ethnic background with a Southerner from a later century, Elvis Presley.

16. Marcus Aurelius Root, *The Camera and the Pencil, or, the Heliographic Art* (Philadelphia, 1864; reprint, Pawlet VT: Helios, 1971). Regarding Root, see Trachtenberg, *Reading American Photographs*, 28–32, 41–42.

17. The Douglass carte-de-visite from the Root studio was by Samuel Root. See Voss, *Majestic in His Wrath*, 71.

18. Quoted in Deborah Willis, *Reflections in "Black": A History of Black Photographers, 1840 to the Present* (New York: W. W. Norton, 2000), xvii.

19. Ellington received the Presidential Medal of Honor on his seventieth birth-

day in 1970. See United States Postal Service, *I Have a Dream: A Collection of Black Americans on U.S. Postage Stamps* (n.p., n.d.), 17.

20. My analysis builds on Hazel Carby's perceptive discussion of Paul Robeson's images in *Race Men* (Cambridge: Harvard University Press, 1998), 45–83. But whereas Carby contrasts the way Nickolas Muray photographed Robeson with how Robeson presented himself (64–66), I contrast the controlling images surrounding Ellington with his own self-fashioning.

21. Joseph Boskin, *Sambo: The Rise and Demise of an American Jester* (New York: Oxford University Press, 1986), 86–89, 167–173.

22. Albert Murray, "Duke Ellington Vamps 'Til Ready,' " in *Chant of Saints: A Gathering of Afro-American Literature, Art, and Scholarship*, ed. Michael S. Harper and Robert B. Stepto (Urbana: University of Illinois Press, 1979), 441. See also Albert Murray, "Ellington Hits 100," *The Nation*, 22 February 1999, 23–29.

23. Several recent studies focus on blackface minstrelsy and stereotype, e.g., Boskin, *Sambo*; Thomas Laurence Riis, *More Than Just Minstrel Shows: The Rise of Black Musical Theatre at the Turn of the Century* (Brooklyn NY: Institute for Studies in American Music, 1992); Eric Lott, *Love and Theft: Blackface Minstrelsy and the American Working Class* (New York: Oxford University Press, 1995); Annemarie Bean, James V. Hatch, and Brooks McNamara, eds., *Inside the Minstrel Mask: Readings in Nineteenth-Century Blackface Minstrelsy* (Hanover NH: Wesleyan University Press, 1996); Dale Cockrell, *Demons of Disorder: Early Blackface Minstrels and Their World* (Cambridge: Cambridge University Press, 1997); W. T. Lhamon Jr., *Raising Cain: Blackface Performance from Jim Crow to Hip Hop* (Cambridge: Harvard University Press,1997); William J. Mahar, *Behind the Burnt Cork Mask: Early Blackface Minstrelsy and AnteBellum American Popular Culture* (Urbana: University of Illinois Press, 1998); and an insightful novel by Wesley Brown, *Darktown Strutters*. (Cane Hill Press, 1994; Amherst: University of Massachusetts, 2000).

24. Quoted from Herman Gray, "Black Masculinity and Visual Culture," *Black: Representations of Masculinity in Contemporary American Art*, ed. Thelma Golden (New York: Whitney Museum of American Art, 1994), 175. See also Henry Louis Gates Jr., "The Trope of a New Negro and the Reconstruction of the Image of the Black," *Representations* 24 (fall 1988): 129–55, and Harry Stecopoulos and Michael Uebel, eds., *Race and the Subject of Masculinities* (Durham: Duke University Press, 1997).

Selected Bibliography

Boskin, Joseph. *Sambo: The Rise and Demise of an American Jester*. New York: Oxford University Press, 1986.

Brilliant, Richard. *Portraiture*. Cambridge: Harvard University Press, 1991.

Collins, Patricia Hill. *Black Feminist Thought: Knowledge, Consciousness, and the Politics of Empowerment*. 2nd ed. New York: Routledge, 2000.

Foner, Philip S. *Frederick Douglass, A Biography*. New York: Citadel Press, 1964.

Gardiner, James. *Who's a Pretty Boy Then? One Hundred and Fifty Years of Gay Life in Pictures*. London: Serpent's Tail, 1996.

Golden, Thelma. *Black: Representations of Masculinity in Contemporary American Art*. New York: Whitney Museum of American Art, 1994.

Harper, Michael S., and Robert B. Stepto, eds. *Chant of Saints: A Gathering of Afro-American Literature, Art, and Scholarship*. Urbana: University of Illinois Press, 1979.

hooks, bell. *Black Looks: Race and Representation*. Boston: South End Press, 1992.

Martin, Waldo E. *The Mind of Frederick Douglass*. Chapel Hill: University of North Carolina Press, 1984.

McFeely, William S. *Frederick Douglass*. New York: W. W. Norton, 1990.

Mitchell, W. J. T. *Iconology: Image, Text, Ideology*. Chicago: University of Chicago Press, 1986.

————, ed. *The Language of Images*. Chicago: University of Chicago Press, 1980.

————, ed. *Picture Theory*. Chicago: University of Chicago Press, 1994.

Quarles, Benjamin. *Frederick Douglass*. Englewood Cliffs NJ: Prentice-Hall, 1968.

Reid-Pharr, Robert F. *Conjugal Union: The Body, the House, and the Black American*. New York: Oxford University Press, 1999.

Rose, Phyllis. *Jazz Cleopatra: Josephine Baker in Her Time*. New York: Doubleday, 1989.

Stafford, Barbara Maria. *Good Looking: Essays on the Virtue of Images*. Cambridge: MIT Press, 1996.

Stecopoulos, Harry, and Michael Uebel, eds. *Race and the Subject of Masculinities*. Durham: Duke University Press, 1997.

Steiner, Wendy. *The Colors of Rhetoric*. Chicago: University of Chicago Press, 1982.

Sundquist, Eric J., ed. *Frederick Douglass: New Literary and Historical Essays*. Cambridge: Cambridge University Press, 1990.

Trachtenberg, Alan. *Reading American Photographs: Images as History, Mathew Brady to Walker Evans*. New York: Hill & Wang, 1989.

Voss, Frederick. *Majestic in His Wrath: A Pictorial Life of Frederick Douglass*. Washington DC: Smithsonian Institution Press for the National Portrait Gallery and the National Park Service, 1995.

Watkins, Mel. *On the Real Side: Laughing, Lying, and Signifying—The Underground Tradition of African American Humor that Transformed American Culture, Slavery to Richard Pryor*. New York: Simon & Schuster, 1994.

Willis, Deborah, ed. *Picturing US: African-American Identity in Photography*. New York: New Press, 1994.

Willis, Deborah. *Reflections in Black: A History of Black Photographers, 1840 to the Present*. New York: W. W. Norton, 2000.

6. Did Friedrich Schelling Kill Auguste Böhmer and Does It Matter? The Necessity of Biography in the History of Philosophy

Robert J. Richards

On 10 August 1802, an anonymous review appeared in the influential journal *Die Allgemeine Literatur-Zeitung*, a journal that was a bit like the *New York Review of Books* for Germany. The reviewer gave an account of a rather obscure pamphlet, "Lob der allerneusten Philosophie"—"Praise of the newest Philosophy." It was a title ironically meant.[1] The broadside reported that a medical candidate, Joseph Reubein, had produced a thesis—very much like that of Friedrich Schelling, the young idealistic philosopher at Jena—that showed how death could be overcome. To the sardonic description of Reubein's views, the author added—and this sentence was prominently quoted in the *Allgemeine Literatur-Zeitung*: "Heaven protect Reubein that he does not meet a patient whom he idealistically cures but really kills—a misfortune that befell Schelling at Bocklet in the case of M. B. as some malicious people say." On reading this, Friedrich Schelling became benumbed with fury and, I suspect, rather depressed with not a little guilt. His first thoughts were to seek judicial action against the ALZ or to go directly to the ducal court for redress. The death to which the review referred was that of Mademoiselle Böhmer—M. B.—Auguste Böhmer. Auguste's death a year and a half earlier had had a cataclysmic effect on Schelling's life, and he obviously still had not gotten over it.[2] Auguste Böhmer was thought by some to have been Schelling's fiancée—probably not, I think. She was, though, the daughter of Schelling's lover, Caroline Böhmer-Schlegel, who at the time of her daughter's death was married to August Wilhelm Schlegel, the great literary critic and one of the founders of the Romantic circle in Jena, of which Schelling himself was a member.

Now, everything that I've mentioned—and I'll try to give a more detailed account in a moment—is typically looked upon by historians of philosophy as overripe gossip—that is, if they themselves even know anything about it, and almost no one does. Bare mention of the incident—something like, for instance, "Schelling is alleged to have killed his fiancée"—might appear in the opening pages of a treatment of Schelling's philosophy, where a description of the philosopher's life is usually potted and planted in a corner, so that the details of the life won't mingle with an exposition of the philosophy. Indeed, almost universally, a discussion of the thought of a philosopher—either in a monograph or as a chapter or two in a general history of philosophy—is conducted in the sanitized space devoted to the philosopher's ideas, ideas not enmeshed in a life but untimely ripped from the life.

A couple of years ago, while I was working on William James, I saw this practice given poignant expression in an essay in which the author urged: "To provide a proper perspective for the study of James . . . attention must be diverted from his life, however interesting, to his published philosophy."[3] Now, just what perspective on an individual could be gained by neglecting the life? James himself, I knew, would have rejected that proposition utterly. It was James, after all, who contended: "The recesses of feeling, the darker, blinder strata of character are the only places in the world in which we catch real fact in the making, and directly perceive how events happen, and how work is actually done."[4] In trying to explain a major shift in James's thought, I found I certainly had to reject the proposition that only the highly polished surface of his ideas needed to be considered. It is this proposition that I would like to argue against even more adamantly today. Put more positively, mine will be basically Fichte's thesis that the kind of philosophy one practices is determined by the kind of person one is.[5] I believe that the intellectual historian—whether of philosophy or of science—must reinsert the ideas, the theories, the intellectual development of an individual into what we think of as a full-bodied life—that is, an existence caught up in the tangle of personal relationships, subject to emotional turmoil, and expressive of hopes and desires—a life that will also be invested in certain approaches to nature and in patterns of logical analysis. But in respect to the latter, the key term will be "invested."

My argument will be local; but, it has, I think, general applicability. I will give an account of a major shift in the thought of Friedrich Schelling, though in terms other than the usual ones. Schelling presents a difficult challenge, yet one, I think, in which a hard case produces good law. He's difficult, since his philosophical ideas are exceedingly abstract and tied together with the sheerest gossamer. It would seem that the mundane events of life could hardly explain alteration in such ethereal speculations. I should say at the beginning that I take it to be the task of the intellectual historian not simply to display what individuals thought, not simply to describe what principles or laws they discovered, but to explain why they thought what they did, and why they altered their views, at least as regards major changes, in their intellectual outlook. Put another way, I think it is the job of the historian not merely to show the development of a series of ideas but to explain them causally, to render those ideas, as best one can, as the absolutely determined outcome of their psychological, social, logical, and natural environments.

There is another task of the intellectual historian, not usually discriminated. The historian, I believe, has to make the reader feel the urgency of certain moments in the life of his or her subject, to raise the pitch of understanding through the energy of the reader's own emotions. So in constructing an explanation of the alterations in the thought of a philosopher or scientist, the historian, deploying all the arts of history, needs to recreate in the reader feelings similar to those that galvanized the subject during the course of that individual's development. It's one thing to say that a person was motivated in action or thought by a burning love or a cold hate; it's quite another to get the reader to feel a little of the sting of those emotions in order to comprehend their power. The historian must construct a narrative to which the reader will give, in Newman's terms, not simply *notional* assent but *real* assent. The medium of historical expression is also the message that, I believe, provides real understanding at a level beyond the notional.

In a short essay, however, much has to be abbreviated, and I fear I'm not quite going to live up to the ideal I've just described.[6] Let me first sketch the problem that I've tried to solve in the history of Schelling's thought, and then use this as a test case. The problem, simply put, is this: Schelling began his philosophical career as an avid and committed disciple of Johann Gottlieb Fichte. But around 1801, he explicitly rejected Fichte's "subjective idealism," as Schelling termed it, for his own "objective idealism," or "ideal-realism." I'm not going to be able, in a short time, I suspect, to make clear all that's at stake in this transition. The philosophical conceptions are notoriously difficult and complex, and Schelling himself was ever attempting to find the right language in which to express these ideas — he often had them more as presentiments, I think, than fully articulated conceptions. In 1799, for instance, he undertook a study of Dante's poetry, since he thought terza rima might be just the vehicle to capture his philosophical vision, so elusive was it. But let me begin at the beginning and sketch quite inadequately both the life and the thought.

Friedrich Wilhelm Joseph Schelling was born in 1775 in a small town outside of Stuttgart, where his father was assistant pastor at the Lutheran church. The father became a professor of religion at the higher seminary in Bebenhausen near Tübingen. There the young Schelling was enrolled as a special student, since he was about five years younger than the other pupils. He was a frighteningly swift learner. Next, at the Tübinger Stift, he began his study of theology, again with students some five years his senior. Schelling had to share a room at the theologate with two other young men whose critical intensity would soon turn brightly stellar, Friedrich Hölderlin, whose poetic talent would soon bloom for all to see, and Georg Wilhelm Friedrich Hegel, who became Germany's greatest philosopher in the early nineteenth century. Though the patron of the school, Duke Karl Eugen of Baden-Würtemberg, tried to seal his wards off from corrupting influences, two powerful waves broke over the walls of the seminary—the French Revolution and the Kantian revolution. In the Germanies, it was a politically exhilarating time, not unlike, I think, the late 1960s in the United States. For Schelling, reading Immanuel Kant and Johann Gottfried Herder began to undermine the standard theology he was fed at the seminary. His dyspepsia is indicated in his first published article, on the nature of myth, with particular examples drawn from the Book of Genesis.[7] This essay appeared when he was eighteen years old. As he lumbered toward the end of his seminary career, he chanced to hear a lecture in June of 1793 by an intellectual firebrand, Johann Gottlieb Fichte. Schelling fell under the spell of this bewitching thinker.

Fichte had argued, in the various versions of his *Wissenschaftslehre*, for what he thought the ineluctable implications of a strict Kantianism—so strict, in fact, that Kant himself would thoroughly reject Fichte's version. Kant, Fichte argued, was correct in reducing the formal structures of experienced reality to the subjective structures of the ego. But had Kant the courage of Fichte's convictions, he would have gone further and shown that no theoretical ground existed for confirming anything beyond the self, certainly no thing-in-itself that might restrict the freedom of the ego. According to Fichte, with the elimination of the thing-in-itself we would have to conclude that all experience resulted from the ego. Even the ego itself, he maintained, was the product of its own self-positing. He argued that all individuals, as soon as they became conscious of the world around them, implicitly had to be conscious of themselves as well, conscious that their representations were connected in a continuous and identical activity of thought. By taking itself up at each moment through self-recognition—what Fichte called "self-positing"—the ego reproduced itself as an identical flow of consciousness. The ego was simply this self-reflective, flowing activity, nothing more—no underlying Cartesian substance that thinks, only the activity itself.[8] Thus the ego was author of itself and its world. As Fichte wrote the philosopher Friedrich Jacobi: "You are a well known realist, and I a transcendental idealist, more uncompromising than Kant was; for he still had as a given a manifold of experience—but God knows how and where it came from. I rather maintain—these are hard words—that the manifold of sense has been produced by us out of our own creative faculty."[9] Well, this was the second phase of the Kantian revolution that ignited Schelling's imagination.

Late in the summer of 1795, Schelling completed his theological studies and then finished with orthodoxy as well. He had no inclination or intention to follow in his father's footsteps. The marker of this resolution appeared in print under the title *Philosophische Briefe über Dogmatismus und Kritizismus*, published when he was only twenty years old. I stress his age, since it makes clear that Schelling was a philosophical Wunderkind, and his reputation as a kind of conceptual Mozart was beginning to take wing. In these *Philosophische Briefe*, he waged a polemic against those pseudo-Kantians—some of his own theology professors—who used the master's moral arguments in an attempt to prove God's existence as a thing-in-itself.[10] With the righteous indignation of the newly converted, he insisted upon the inconceivability and the contradictions involved in any reference to a thing-in-itself. Schelling's rejection of the route for which his seminary days had prepared him meant only one real possibility for his immediate future—academic servitude.

Schelling became a tutor to the family of the very wealthy Baron von Riedesel in Stuttgart. He followed his two young wards to the University of Leipzig to help them in their study of law, which meant that Schelling himself had to learn the law first. While at Leipzig he also attended lectures in a variety of natural sciences, including medicine, which he thought he could completely master in a few years—at least that's what he told his parents.[11] During the two years that he was occupied as tutor, he completed several large philosophical tracts, which made his reputation incandescent. The most durable of these tracts was his *Ideen zu einer Philosophie der Natur*, published in 1797.[12] In this book, Schelling attempted to carry out the second phase of the Fichtean project. The first phase, with which Schelling would continue to occupy himself, was the effort to derive from the structures of the ego the basic features of experience, including its material content. The second phase, one that Fichte himself never bothered about, was *Naturphilosophie*. Schelling's *Naturphilosophie* had the task of beginning with a refined understanding of nature, that is, a nature articulated with the help of the latest empirical, scientific theories—those, for instance, of Antoine-Laurent de Lavoisier in chemistry and Alexander von Humboldt in electrophysiology—and then of showing how these scientifically construed natural phenomena and their relationships could be regressively chased back into the ego as their only possible source. Schelling's *Ideen* became the fundamental document for *romantische Naturphilosophie* during the first quarter of the nineteenth century.

The signal idea to which the other Romantics resonated was the proposal that the absolute ego created both the empirical ego and nature in reciprocal relation. Under this conception, to explore nature, to understand nature, was simply to understand the self. This relationship between nature and the self, however, could be comprehended not only by scientific investigation of nature but also by aesthetic appreciation of mind in nature. As Schelling put it a few years later: "The objective world is simply the original, though unconscious, poetry of the mind [*Geist*]."[13] These ideas, which would become the core of the Romantic legacy, had a tremendous effect on Schelling's contemporaries—philosophical, scientific, and literary—in both Germany and England. Alexander von Humboldt, for instance, endorsed Schelling's metaphysics, for he realized that when he went into the jungles of South America, to which he traveled in 1799, he had discovered in those exotic climes the self that he truly was. Samuel Taylor Coleridge, the great English Romantic poet, simply palmed off large parts of Schelling's *Ideen* as his own in his *Biographia literaria*.

Because of Schelling's several astounding publications, certain individuals at Jena, Fichte principal among them, wanted to get him a position at the university. The main obstacle to his appointment, and initially a barrier the size of the Harz Mountains, was Johann Wolfgang von Goethe, who, as privy counselor to the duke of Saxe-Weimar, could promote or thwart such an appointment. Goethe read Schelling's *Ideen*, and he balked. Goethe wrote to Friedrich Schiller, the great poet who was teaching at Jena:

> On reading Schelling's book [*Ideen*], I've had other thoughts, which we must more thoroughly pursue. I gladly grant that it is not nature that we know, but that she is taken up by us according to certain forms and abilities of our mind. . . . [Yet] you know how closely I hold to the idea of the internal purposiveness [*Zweckmässigkeit*] of organic nature. . . . Let the idealist attack things-in-themselves as he wishes, he will yet stumble on things outside himself before he anticipates them; and, as it seems to me, they always cross him up at the first meeting, just as the Chinese is nonplussed by the chaffing dish.[14]

Goethe thoroughly disliked the suggestion that nature was nonobjective, not thoroughly real, lacking her own peculiar ways. He was not going to help in the appointment. Schiller, however, engineered a wine soiree to which both Goethe and Schelling were invited. The great poet was unexpectedly charmed by the young philosopher. The Schelling he met had, as Goethe wrote to a friend, "a very clear, energetic, and, according to the latest fashion, a well-organized head on his shoulders." And below the shoulders, as he assured his friend, the minister Voigt, the young man gave "no hint of being a sansculotte"—unlike Fichte, presumably, whom many at Jena thought a Jacobin.[15] Goethe was surprised at his new friend's knowledge of optics, and the two spoke for hours on the topic, undoubtedly boring the other guests. Schelling likely let slip a few knowing references to Goethe's recently published *Beiträge zur Optik*, which he had lately been reading. Goethe became a convert, and quickly interceded on Schelling's behalf. As a result, on 30 June 1798, the twenty-three-year-old tutor received a call to Jena as *extraodinarius* professor of philosophy.

During his first year at Jena, Schelling mostly associated with Fichte, Schiller, and Goethe. But during the next year, Fichte's very spiny relationships beyond this circle drew their final blood. Fichte had irritated his colleagues at the university by holding lectures on Sunday mornings, during the time of church services. He had also irritated the *Burschenschaften*—the student fraternities—by complaining about their drinking and rowdiness; they retaliated by breaking his windows. Goethe wryly observed in his diary that having a stone thrown through your window was "the most unpleasant way to become convinced of the existence of the not-I."[16] Finally, Fichte irritated Duke Karl August of Saxe-Weimar, at whose pleasure he served in the university. Fichte's views on God were highly unorthodox, amounting in the minds of many to atheism, which the duke would not tolerate. In 1799 Fichte was dismissed from the university.

With Fichte's departure, Schelling began to associate more and more with those in the circle around Wilhelm Schlegel—the literary critic, translator, and a cofounder of the group that became known as the Early Romantics, or Jena Romantics. This group included the poet Friedrich von Hardenberg (who wrote under the pen name of Novalis); Friedrich

Schlegel, the younger brother of Wilhelm—he was a philosopher, poet, and critic, and the real force behind the Romantic circle; Dorothea Veit (daughter of Moses Mendelssohn), a married woman who had just come to live with Friedrich Schlegel at Jena; Ludwig Tieck, the novelist—acerbically funny, and the light spirit of the circle; and finally, the very beautiful, charming, intriguing Caroline Böhmer-Schlegel, who was married to Wilhelm Schlegel. I have to say a few words about Caroline.

Caroline Michaelis was born in Göttingen in 1763, the daughter of Johann David Michaelis, the famous biblical scholar and orientalist. When she was twenty, she was married off to a country doctor, Georg Böhmer, who took her to a little mountain village, where she bore him three children; only her daughter Auguste survived infancy. In the small village, she had been excruciatingly bored. Mercifully, after three years in this stultifying town, her husband died. She gratefully returned with Auguste to Göttingen, where she met and toyed with the affections of Wilhelm Schlegel, who was a student at Göttingen—toyed because, though fond of him, she had fallen deeply in love with another man. After receiving his degree, Schlegel had to leave Germany for Amsterdam to take up a tutorial post; but he kept in correspondence with this woman, with whom he had fallen utterly in love. Caroline, in 1792, moved with her daughter Auguste to Mainz to be near her childhood friend Therese Heyme. Therese lived there with her husband Georg Forster. Forster was heavily engaged in republican politics and became a leader of the revolutionary group at Mainz. He inducted Caroline into political work, having her translate letters of Mirabeau and Condorcet. Her feelings for Forster spanned a wide range. She later wrote a friend during the difficult time of the French occupation of Mainz: "He is the most wonderful man; there is no one I have so loved or admired, or, again, thought so little of."[17]

During the spring of 1792, Austria and Prussia planned a nice little war with the new French Republic, since that government seemed to be in chaos in wake of the Revolution. Well, not so chaotic that the French Assembly couldn't anticipate the Germans and strike first. In April the French declared war against the Germanies. Initially, the troops of Austria, Prussia, and the many dukedoms of the German lands captured several French cities on the way to Paris. However, unaccountably, the French didn't collapse and return to the ancient order. The initial wave of German successes finally crashed against debilitating dysentery, shortage of food, and a regrouped French force, which now began moving the enemy armies out of France and back into Germany. Indeed, the French troops began taking German cities in the Rhineland, and finally Mainz fell. Forster's wife, Therese, with their two children, abandoned the city; but Forster remained to help establish a new democratic government. He thus dared treason, braced only with an enlightened faith in democracy and Caroline Böhmer by his side. Caroline moved into his house to help secure the new dispensation, and thus herself became, in the eyes of the opposing German authorities, a dangerous and degenerate traitor.

During the French occupation of Mainz, Caroline had a brief liaison with a French lieutenant, Jean Baptiste Dubois Crancé. It lasted only about a month and a half. He had to depart in advance of the counterattacking German armies. The city was put under siege, but Caroline escaped with Auguste. However, on the way back to Braunschweig, where her mother now lived, they were captured. Caroline was thought to be the mistress of Forster—she was called the whore of the Revolution. She was thrown into prison with her daughter. In these wretched conditions, with many of the Mainz revolutionaries going to the gallows just outside her cell, she discovered that she was pregnant with the French lieutenant's child. In this pitiable state, she wrote to all her friends and those of her father. Wilhelm von Humboldt and her brother Philip bargained with the Prussian king for her release. Meanwhile, the faithful Wilhelm Schlegel rushed to her side with the poison she had requested, to end her misery and her disgrace. Before she could take the fatal draught, she was released on her brother's bond and promise. Schlegel brought her to Leipzig, and there arranged for his brother, Friedrich, to care for her during her pregnancy, while he returned to Amsterdam to earn the money necessary to keep them all going.

Friedrich Schlegel, who would be the instigator of the Romantic movement in Jena, was a man of remarkable intellectual gifts, with a genius for love, and, as it turned out, hate. Friedrich fell deeply in love with this pregnant radical, the woman he thought destined for his own brother. He stayed with Caroline through her pregnancy and the baptism of the infant, whom Friedrich referred to as the little Citizen Wilhelm Julius Cranz; the child died shortly after baptism.

Caroline returned with her daughter to her mother's house in Braunschweig, and in July 1795 Wilhelm Schlegel came from Amsterdam to be with them. Caroline wrote Friedrich Schlegel that his brother now preferred to speak and write in French and that he "thinks differently of my friends, the republicans, and is certainly no longer an aristocrat. . . . And I will soon teach him passion—then will my instruction be complete."[18] The next year the instruction seemed to have taken, for they married, and then immediately moved to Jena, where Schlegel had been called to the university. Caroline helped in her husband's literary ventures, commenting on his translations of Shakespeare into German and even writing some essays under his name. Their home became a favorite meeting place for friends sharing their temperament, which did not include the misogynistic Friedrich Schiller. He still regarded Caroline as a dangerous radical, and later referred to her as Madam Lucifer. When Friedrich Schlegel came from Berlin with his new love, Dorothea, along with Ludwig Tieck, and with Novalis living close by, the salon of the Schlegels was the place to be. And Schelling was there. They would gather in the evenings with some good wine and cold beef, as Friedrich Schlegel put it, "to sympoetize and symphilosophize, and yes to symlaze-about."[19] This group of friends constituted the Jena Romantics, and their interactions gave rise to the literary, philosophical, and scientific movement of that name.

From the beginning, Caroline found the young philosopher Schelling—he was twelve years her junior—to be a fascinating intellect, and more. Initially they waged the typical sexual-intellectual wars that bespoke an underlying deeper attraction. She gave an account of their preliminary skirmishes to Novalis in a letter in the fall of 1799: "Concerning Schelling, no one ever dropped so impenetrable a veil. And though I cannot be together with him more than six minutes without a fight breaking out, he is far and away the most interesting person I know. I wish we would see him more often and more intimately. Then there really would be a wrangle. He is constantly wary of me and the irony of the Schlegel family. He is always rather tense, and I have not yet found the secret to loosen him up.

Recently we celebrated his twenty-fourth birthday. He has time to become more relaxed."[20]

The bantering battles between Caroline and Schelling gradually faded into a deep love. She would later pour out her feelings: "I am yours, I love you, I revere you, no hour passes that I do not think of you."[21] As the relationship between Caroline and Schelling gradually took form, that between Caroline and Dorothea quickly came undone. Caroline was obviously the star of their little society—beautiful, vivacious, demanding, creative, smart—a mélange of the traits that make intellectual men pliable and careful women distrustful. The tensions within the community reached a breaking point when Schelling consented to follow Caroline to Bamberg, where she was to consult the doctors about a minor but lingering illness. Neither Friedrich Schlegel, nor Dorothea, nor certainly her husband Wilhelm regarded Schelling's offer to accompany Caroline as an example of pure altruism. By this time, Friedrich Schlegel had turned against Caroline, undoubtedly because of his own dying love and for the sake of his brother. Dorothea became reserved, cool, and proper, as she explained in a letter to her friend Friedrich Schleiermacher, back in Berlin:

> My entire manner with Caroline lies right on the border of common civility. Each day I make one or two short visits, but turn aside any closer relationship, since she is Friedrich's enemy, so why should I be concerned?—She takes daily walks with Auguste and Schelling, but that does little good, she says, so that a complete change of place will be necessary for her fully to recover. She will, therefore, travel this week with Schelling to Bamberg and there take the required baths. . . . They will leave shortly, and we'll be able to breath again. I doubt that she'll quickly return, perhaps never! But she indicated to Wilhelm that she would soon come back—just so that she wouldn't completely leave him, or he her.[22]

Caroline consulted with the doctors at Bamberg and traveled with Auguste, who had just turned fifteen, to Bocklet, close by, to take the baths. Schelling, in the meantime, had left for a quick visit with his parents. When he returned to Bocklet, he found Caroline better, but Auguste now ill, apparently with typhus. The local doctor promised an easy recovery in a few days. But on 12 July 1800, Auguste, Caroline's most beloved daughter, a young woman of infinite grace, refined education, and lively charm, suddenly died. Caroline was devastated. When he heard the news, Wilhelm, Auguste's stepfather, wrote to Tieck that "it was as if I had stored all my tears for this, and at times I have the feeling that I should completely dissolve into tears."[23] Henrik Steffens, a disciple of Schelling who had fallen for Auguste, wrote an anguished letter to his mentor. He mentioned that he was sending his letter without stopping to correct anything. He wrote:

> I cannot bear to say what for me, yes, for me, what Auguste's loss means. That beautiful—I cannot grasp her death.—So full of life, so much promise—and now dead. I can't speak about it—Oh! She was more dear to me than anyone knows, more than I want to confess. . . . When I am able to work in peace, when healthy and in a good frame of mind, I consider everything that Jena has meant to me, the source of my higher life, that child stands before me like a bright angel. When I was last in Jena, she became even closer to me—and now. Never—never, after so many years, has death come so close to me—I've seen accidents and people die, but saw only change. I didn't see death—and now—well, I shouldn't renew the pain. Greet the unhappy mother for me.[24]

Dorothea's response didn't touch quite the same emotional depths. She characterized Auguste's death as a "sacrificial offering for sin."[25] Schelling, however, went into collapse. He reached such depths that Caroline wrote Goethe from her mother's home in Braunschweig to plead with him to care for the young philosopher, who, she said, had "suffered so much in body and soul."[26] She was afraid, it seems, that he would commit suicide. Goethe quickly acquiesced and invited Schelling to spend the Christmas holidays with him. It is hard to believe that Schelling was not in love with Auguste as much as with Caroline. The conclusion is easy to draw, since everyone seemed to be in love with her, including her uncle Friedrich. The pitch of Schelling's response, however, had a sharper curve, since he was blamed for her death—and he did suffer despairing guilt. Immediately Dorothea gossiped that Caroline and her lover had not called in a proper doctor when Auguste became ill and that Schelling had meddled (*pfuschet*) in the treatment.[27] And, indeed, he did alter the treatment prescribed by the doctor.

When Schelling returned from visiting his parents at the beginning of July, he found Auguste ill. He called in a local doctor, who followed the Brownian medical practice. The doctor prescribed opium mixed with gum arabic and tincture of rhubarb. The rhubarb was presumably to moderate the constipation that opium would induce. Schelling removed the gum and rhubarb from the prescription—he thought them too much an emetic for her condition—and saw to it that the opium was in a smaller dose than originally recommended. Actually, all of this was probably a wise move, since typhus kills through dehydration. But Schelling did confess to Wilhelm Schlegel that he felt terribly guilty because he had trusted the local physician.[28] These circumstances were sufficient—and the moral offense at his relations with Caroline so heated—that rumors of his culpability took wing, eventually bringing the charge that appeared in the *Allgemeine Literatur-Zeitung*, quoted at the beginning of this essay.

During the time that Schelling bore the considerable weight of his affair with Caroline—and it eventuated in her divorce from her husband Wilhelm Schlegel and her marriage to Schelling in 1803—during this time, when he also felt the crushing guilt, however unwarranted, for the death of Auguste, he was moving toward a break with his mentor Fichte. Though Schelling initially endorsed Fichte's epistemological and metaphysical conception that everything exists for and in the ego, his scientific work and his developing ideas about the independence of natural phenomena moved him slowly away from that starting point. Nevertheless, as late as March 1800 he proclaimed, in his *System des transzendentalen Idealismus*, that his position was essentially the same as that of the author of the *Wissenschaftslehre*.

But during this time of reconsideration of his philosophical stance, from the beginning of 1801, Schelling interpreted Fichte's absolute ego as an individual subject—one of many such subjects; and as such it, too, needed to be explained, not simply assumed. Schelling now believed that the explanation had to invoke an absolute, a state that was neither subject nor object, but both indifferently—something akin to Spinoza's *Deus sive Natura*—whence individual egos and their world would emanate. Methodologically, this meant that Fichte's subjective idealism had to be subordinated to the one-time disciple's new objective idealism. As Schelling expressed it in January 1801, casting a mirror image of his earlier position: "There is an idealism of nature and an idealism of the ego. The former is for me the original, the latter derived."[29]

The precipitating causes of the split between Schelling and Fichte, I believe, were manifold. They ranged from bitter feelings over intellectual politics to the solace of reconciling love, from a desire for professional independence to the recognition of subtle intellectual differences, and from the experience of the autonomy of science to the remorse over the death of a beloved.

The growing intellectual differences felt by Schelling, and his appreciation of the logic separating his theory from Fichte's are typically noted by historians of philosophy. I do not think, however, that these intellectual factors would have had purchase on the mind of the young philosopher had he and Fichte not been caught in the matrix of the other causes. What might seem trivially mundane and personal to a more purified ideal of philosophical comportment, I nonetheless believe, had epistemological and metaphysical consequences.

Fichte's subjectivism made occurrences in the natural world—including the unreasonable demands of love and the more unreasonable death of a young girl of splendid promise—somehow the ultimate responsibility of the ego. And from the emotional perspective—despite the logic of the situation—the responsible ego had to be Schelling's. A subjective idealism made other individuals solipsistically the productive responsibility of the self. A young philosopher, closed off in his study and communicating to his students only from the high chair of the German professorate, might imagine a world only of his own making and with an imperious gesture take responsibility for it. But that same philosopher, now pulled down by the grappling hooks of love and then dashed against the rocks of his own conscience by the death of a beautiful spirit, must, I think, have his isolated self torn asunder. Only the abandonment of Fichtean egoism and the adoption of an austere and deterministic absolutism might mitigate the responsibility for love and for death—or so, I believe, the emotional dialectic would have proceeded.

And wouldn't that emotional fuel be required to alter the path that one might take through a logical maze of ideas? That is, seen from the jejune perspective usually attained by scholars writing the history of philosophy or science, bare ideas have, I think, no power to urge one this way or that. From this perspective, ideas, as David Hume, for instance, portrayed them, are completely effete, impotent. Schelling, simply from the logical point of view, could have stayed on the path originally cut by Fichte, a path he seemed content with as late as March 1800. Nothing in the antecedent ideas per se required him to move as he had. Certainly the logical thicket became no less dense along the path he finally took; rather, it was fraught with more difficulties. Schelling needed emotional fuel and direction to propel him one way rather than another. His love of Caroline—certainly the arrow that pierced the solipsistic Fichtean ego to convince him of a reality beyond the self—and the death of Auguste—a burden impossible for a lonely ego to bear—provided, I think, both the impetus and the direction for his change of philosophical position.

The final push came from Caroline. She wrote Schelling in March 1801, as their desperate love hardened into an impervious shield against the world:

> It occurs to me that for all Fichte's incomparable power of thought, his powerful mode of drawing conclusions, his clarity, exactness, his direct intuition of the ego and the inspiration of the discoverer, that he is yet limited. . . . When you have broken through a barrier that he has not yet overcome, then I have to believe that you have accomplished this, not so much as a philosopher—if I'm using this term incorrectly, don't scold me—but rather because you have poetry and he has none. It leads you directly to production, while the sharpness of his perception leads him to consciousness. He has light in its most bright brightness, but you also have warmth; the former can only enlighten, while the latter is productive. . . . In my opinion, Spinoza must have had far more poetry than Fichte—if thought isn't tinctured with it, doesn't something lifeless remain therein?[30]

I believe Caroline was correct. Without the poetical and affective configuration of ideas, which give direction and power to those ideas, something lifeless does remain therein. Schelling's own ideas could hardly have found a more loving efflation to lift them from the reflective plane of possibility and send them on the trajectory they actually took. Three months after receiving that letter, Schelling quickly published his *Darstellung meines Systems der Philosophie*, which explicitly signaled his break with Fichte.

What I've tried to show in this essay is the general proposal concerning the nature of intellectual history, namely that ideas must be pulled along by more than merely logical cords. After all, from a set of premises, an infinite number of conclusions can be drawn, but only a finite trail can be taken. What, then, will force the decision to take one permissible path rather than another? I think it will be the usual springs of action—the interests, passions, and desires that can be comprehended only by unraveling the fabric of a life, rather than merely by dissecting abstract ideas. The historian has to unknot the skein, so that all the strands can be appreciated. But to be convincing, the good historian will also reweave the threads to touch the emotions of readers, so that they might feel something of the forces that drove the actors to take one path rather than another. I think that's the only way to produce real conviction, rather than simply notional assent.

To answer, then, the question of my title: Yes, Auguste's death, and all that it represented, mattered a great deal to Schelling's life—and to his philosophy, as well as to my general thesis.

Notes

1. Anonymous review of "Lob der allerneusten Philosophie," *Allgemeine Literatur-Zeitung*, no. 225, 10 August 1802, 329.

2. The screed against Schelling was more than a veiled protest against the untimely death of a young girl. Franz Berg, author of the *Lob der allerneusten Philosophie*, was a religiously conservative theologian who connected Schelling's ideas with those of the atheist Fichte. And Berg and Schütz, editor of the ALZ, also reacted against the Brownian medical theories and the Romantic attitudes that supported those views.

3. William Earle, "William James," *The Encyclopedia of Philosophy*, ed. Paul Edwards, 8 vols. (New York: Macmillan, 1967), 4:241.

4. William James, *The Varieties of Religious Experience*, ed. Frederick Burkhardt et al. (Cambridge: Harvard University Press, 1985), 395.

5. Johann Gottlieb Fichte, "Erste Einleitung in die Wissenschaftslehre" (1797), *Fichtes Werke*, ed. Immanuel Hermann Fichte, 11 vols. (Berlin: Walter de Gruyter, [1834–1846] 1971), 1:432–34: "There is no principle of decision possible for reason: for it is not a question of adding an item in a series according to the rational principles governing the series; rather it is a question of the beginning of the whole series which, as an absolute first act, depends only on freedom of thought. . . . What kind of philosophy one chooses thus depends on what kind of man one is: for a philosophical system is not a dead stick of furniture that one can lay aside or select; rather it animates the very soul of the man who has it."

6. I treat Schelling's difficulties more extensively in my *Romantic Conception of Life: Science and Philosophy in the Age of Goethe* (Chicago: University of Chicago Press, 2002).

7. Friedrich Schelling, *Über Mythen, historische Sagen und Philosopheme der Ältesten Welt*, in *Schellings Werke* (Münchner Jubilaumsdruck), ed. Manfred Schroter, 12 vols. (Munich: C. H. Beck, 1927–1959), 1:1–44.

8. Fichte works out these ideas in a treatise he composed between 1794 and 1795. See Johann Gottlieb Fichte, *Grundlage der gesamten Wissenschaftslehre*, in *Fichtes Werke*, 1:83–328.

9. Johann Gottlieb Fichte to Friedrich Jacobi, 30 August 1795, *Johann Gottlieb Fichte, Briefe*, ed. Manfred Buhr, 2nd ed. (Leipzig: Verlag Philip Reclam, 1986), 183–84.

10. Friedrich W. J. Schelling, *Philosophische Briefe über Dogmatismus und Kritizismus*, in *Schellings Werke*, ed. Schroter, 1:205–66.

11. Friedrich Schelling to his parents, 4 September 1797, *F. W. J. Schelling. Briefe und Dokumente*, ed. Horst Fuhrmans, 3 vols. to date (Bonn: H. Bouvier, 1962-), 2:122.

12. Friedrich Schelling, *Ideen zu einer Philosophie der Natur als Einleitung in das Studium dieser Wissenschaft* (1797), in *Schellings Werke*, ed. Schroter, 1:77–350.

13. Friedrich Schelling, *System des transzendentalen Idealismus*, in *Schellings Werke*, ed. Schroter, 2:349.

14. Johann Wolfgang von Goethe to Friedrich Schiller, 6 January 1798, *Der Briefwechsel zwischen Schiller und Goethe*, ed. Emil Staiger (Frankfurt: Insel Verlag, 1966), 537–38.

15. Johann Wolfgang von Goethe to Christian Gottlieb Voigt, 29 May 1798,

Goethes Briefe und Briefe an Goethe (Hamberger Ausgabe), ed. Karl Mandelkow, 6 vols. (Munich: C. H. Beck, 1988), 2:349.

16. Johann Wolfgang von Goethe, *Tag- und Jahres-Hefte* (1796), in *Samtliche Werke nach Epochen seines Schaffens* (Münchner Ausgabe), ed. Karl Richter et al., 21 vols. (Munich: Carl Hanser Verlag, 1985–1998), 14:41.

17. Caroline Böhmer to Friedrich Meyer, 17 December 1792, *Caroline: Briefe aus der Frühromantik*, 2 vols., ed. Georg Waiz and expanded by Erich Schmidt (Leipzig: Insel Verlag, 1913), 1:279.

18. Caroline Böhmer to Friedrich Schlegel, August 1795, in *Caroline: Briefe aus der Frühromantik*, 1:36–67.

19. See the Foreword to *Friedrich Schlegel, 1794–1802: Seine prosaischen Jugenschriften*, ed. J. Minor, 2 vols. (Vienna: Carl Konegen, 1882), v.

20. Caroline Böhmer-Schlegel to Friedrich Hardenberg, 4 February 1799, *Caroline: Briefe aus der Frühromantik*, 1:497.

21. Caroline Böhmer-Schlegel to Friedrich Schelling, February 1801, *Caroline: Briefe aus der Frühromantik*, 2:42.

22. Dorothea Veit to Friedrich Schleiermacher, 28 April 1800, *Friedrich Daniel Ernst Schleiermacher, Kritische Gesamtausgabe*, ed. Han-Joachim Birkner et al., 11 vols. to date (Berlin: Walter de Gruyter, 1980-), 5.4:9.

23. August Wilhelm Schlegel to Ludwig Tieck, 14 September 1800, quoted in Gisela Dischner, *Caroline und der Jenaer Kreis* (Berlin: Verlag Klaus Wagenbach, 1979), 154.

24. Henrik Steffens to Friedrich Schelling, 20 August 1800, in Gustav Plitt, *Aus Schellings Leben. In Briefen*, 3 vols. (Leipzig: S. Hirzel, 1869–1870), 1:305. Steffens's reaction to Auguste's death, as his letter to Schelling indicates, was obviously profound. His deep affection for Auguste can also be gleaned from Caroline's characterization of his behavior with her daughter, which she communicated to Johann Diederich Gries, a Privatdozent in Philosophy at Jena and a friend of several in the circle. See Caroline Böhmer-Schlegel to Johann Diederich Gries, 27 December 1799, *Caroline, Briefe aus der Frühromantik*, 1:592–94.

25. Dorothea Veit to Friedrich Schleiermacher, 28 July 1800, *Schleiermacher, Kritische Gesamtausgabe*, 5.4:175.

26. Caroline Böhmer-Schlegel to Wolfgang von Goethe, 26 November 1800, *Caroline, Briefe aus der Frühromantik*, 2:19.

27. Dorothea Veit to Friedrich Schleiermacher, 22 August 1800, in *Schleiermacher, Kritische Gesamtausgabe*, 5.4:222. Dorothea maintained that Caroline treated Auguste as an adult much too soon, which, along with Caroline's affair with

Schelling, had a debilitating effect. She went on to say: "The Brownian technique, in this case, is not to blame. They had no physician with her other than a completely unknown man from the region of Bocklet, who was no less than a Brownian. To top the whole thing off, Schelling meddled in it [hinein gepfuscht]. They sent for a physician from Bamberg only as she grew cold from the waist up. Röschlaub came and found her already dead. He maintained that her sickness was lethal right from the beginning; all the more unforgivable, then, is the confidence they showed in not sending for a doctor right from the beginning. Shortly—And now the ostentation of the sorrow!—We are going to remain completely silent about all those people. I won't write you anything more on this, since I am simply too indignant."

28. Friedrich Schelling to Wilhelm Schlegel, 3 September 1802, in *F. W. J. Schelling, Briefe und Dokumente*, 2:432.

29. Friedrich Schelling, *Über den wahren Begriff der Naturphilosophie und die richtige Art, ihre Probleme aufzulösen*, in *Schellings Werke*, 2:718.

30. Caroline Böhmer-Schlegel to Friedrich Schelling, 1 March 1801, *Caroline, Briefe aus der Frühromantik*, 2:58.

Selected Bibliography

Berg, Franz. *Lob der allerneusten Philosophie*. Halle: Unbekannt, 1802.

Dischner, Gisela. *Caroline und der Jenaer Kreis*. Berlin: Verlag Klaus Wagenback, 1979.

Earle, William. "William James." *The Encyclopedia of Philosophy*. vol. 4. Edited by Paul Edwards. 8 vols. New York: Macmillan, 1967.

Fichte, Johann Gottlieb. *Fichtes Werke*. Edited by Immanuel Hermann Fichte. 11 vols. Berlin: Walter de Gruyter, 1971 [1834–1846].

———. *Briefe*. Edited by Manfred Buhr. 2nd ed. Leipzig: Reclam, 1986.

Goethe, Johann Wolfgang von. *Stimtliche Werke nach Epochen seines Schaffens* (Münchner Ausgabe). Edited by Karl Richter et al. 21 vols. Munich: Carl Hanser Verlag, 1985–1998.

———. *Goethes Briefe und Briefe an Goethe* (Hamburger Ausgabe). Edited Karl Mandelkow. 6 vols. Munich: C. H. Beck, 1988.

———. *Der Briefwechsel zwischen Schiller und Goethe*. Edited by Emil Staiger. Frankfurt: Insel Verlag, 1966.

James, William. *The Varieties of Religious Experience*. Edited by Frederick Burkhardt et al. Cambridge: Harvard University Press, 1985.

Plitt, Gustav. *Aus Schellings Leben*. 3 vols. Leipzig: S. Hirzel, 1869–1870.

"Review of 'Lob der allerneusten Philosophie.'" *Allgemeine Literatur-Zeitung*. no. 225 (10 August 1802): 329.

Richards, Robert J. *The Romantic Conception of Life: Science and Philosophy in the Age of Goethe*. Chicago: University of Chicago Press, 2002.

Schelling, Friedrich Wilhelm Joseph. *Briefe und Dokumente*. Edited by Horst Fuhrmans. 3 vols. to date. Bonn: Bouvier Verlag, 1962–1975.

———. *Schellings Werke*. Edited by Manfred Schröter. 3rd ed. 14 vols. Munich: Beck'sche Verlagsbuchhandlung, 1979.

Schlegel, Friedrich. *Friedrich Schlegel, 1794–1802: Seine prosaischen Jugendschriften*. Edited by Jacob Minor. 2 vols. Vienna: Carl Konegen, 1882.

Schleiermacher, Friedrich. *Friedrich Daniel Ernst Schleiermacher, Kritische Gesamtausgabe*. Edited by Hans-Joachim Birkner et al. 11 vols. to date. Berlin: Walter de Gruyter, 1980-.

Waitz, Georg, and Erich Schmidt, eds. *Caroline: Briefe aus der Frühromantik*. 2 vols. Leipzig: Insel Verlag, 1913.

Contributors

LLOYD E. AMBROSIUS is professor of history at the University of Nebraska–Lincoln. He is the author of *Woodrow Wilson and the American Diplomatic Tradition: The Treaty Fight in Perspective* (Cambridge University Press, 1987), *Wilsonian Statecraft: Theory and Practice of Liberal Internationalism during World War I* (Scholarly Resources, 1991), and *Wilsonianism: Woodrow Wilson and His Legacy in American Foreign Relations* (Palgrave Macmillan, 2002). He is editor of *The Crisis of Republicanism: American Politics in the Civil War Era* (University of Nebraska Press, 1990). He was the Mary Ball Washington Professor of American History at University College, Dublin, Ireland, and twice a Fulbright Professor at the Universities of Cologne and Heidelberg, Germany.

JOHN MILTON COOPER JR. is the E. Gorton Fox Professor of American Institutions at the University of Wisconsin–Madison. A native of Washington DC, and a graduate of Princeton and Columbia Universities, he previously taught at Wellesley College. He is the author of *The Vanity of Power: American Isolationism and the First World War* (Greenwood Press, 1969), *Walter Hines Page: The Southerner as American, 1855–1918* (University of North Carolina Press, 1977), *The Warrior and the Priest: Woodrow Wilson and Theodore Roosevelt* (Harvard University Press, 1983), *Pivotal Decades: The United States, 1900–1920* (W. W. Norton, 1990), and *Breaking the Heart of the World: Woodrow Wilson and the Fight for the League of Nations* (Cambridge University Press, 2001).

SHIRLEY A. LECKIE is professor of history at the University of Central Florida, where she teaches Women in American History and History of the Trans-Mississippi West among other courses. She is the author of *Angie Debo: Pioneering Historian* (University of Oklahoma Press, 2000) and *Elizabeth Bacon Custer and the Making of a Myth* (University of Oklahoma Press, 1993). She edited *The Colonel's Lady on the Western Frontier: The Correspondence of Alice Kirk Grierson* as a volume in the University of Nebraska Press Women in the West Series in 1989. She is also coauthor of *Unlikely Warriors: General Benjamin Grierson and His Family* (University of Oklahoma Press, 1984).

NELL IRVIN PAINTER is the Edward Professor of American History at Princeton University. She received her Ph.D. at Harvard University after undergraduate and graduate study at the University of California, Berkeley, the University of Bordeaux, the University of Ghana, and the University of California, Los Angeles. Before moving to Princeton, she taught at the University of Pennsylvania and the University of North Carolina, Chapel Hill. The author of five books, including *Standing at Armageddon: The United States, 1877–1919* (W. W. Norton, 1987) and *Sojourner Truth, A Life, A Symbol* (W. W. Norton, 1996), she is also the editor of two Penguin Classic women's ex-slave narratives. Her most recent book is *Southern History Across the Color Line* (University of North Carolina, 2002).

ROBERT J. RICHARDS is professor of history, philosophy, and psychology at the University of Chicago, where he is director of the Fishbein Center for the History of Science. He is the author of *Darwin and the Emergence of Evolutionary Theories of Mind and Behavior* (University of Chicago Press, 1987), *The Meaning of Evolution* (University of Chicago Press, 1992), and *The Romantic Conception of Life: Science and Philosophy in the Age of Goethe* (University of Chicago Press, 2002).

R. KEITH SCHOPPA is the Edward and Catherine Doehler Chair in Asian History at Loyola College in Maryland. He is the author of six books on China, one of which, *Blood Road: The Mystery of Shen Dingyi in Revolutionary China* (University of California Press, 1995), was awarded the 1997 Association for Asian Studies Levenson Prize for the best book on twentieth-century China. He has been a Fellow of the John Simon Guggenheim Foundation, the National Endowment for the Humanities, the American Council of Learned Societies, and the East-West Center.

RETHA M. WARNICKE, who earned a Ph.D. from Harvard University, is professor of history at Arizona State University. She is the author of *Women of the English Renaissance and Reformation* (Greenwood Press, 1983), *The Rise and Fall of Anne Boleyn: Family Politics at the Court of Henry VIII* (Cambridge University Press, 1989), and *The Marrying of Anne of Cleves: Royal Protocol in Tudor England* (Cambridge University Press, 2000). With Bettie Anne Doebler, she has written introductions to five volumes of Englishwomen's funeral sermons, published by Scholars' Facsimilies & Reprints, 1993–2001.

Index

Page numbers in italics refer to illustrations.